TEENS ~ DISCOVERING IDENTITY AND MOVING TOWARD INDEPENDENCE

Facilitator Reproducible
Activities for Groups
and Individuals

Ester R.A. Leutenberg

Carol Butler, MS Ed, RN, C

Illustrated by
Amy L. Brodsky, LISW-S

publisher of therapy, counseling, and self-help resources

Whole Person Associates
101 W. 2nd St., Suite 203
Duluth, MN 55802

800-247-6789

Books@WholePerson.com
WholePerson.com

Teens – Discovering Identity and Moving Toward Independence
Facilitator Reproducible Activities for Groups and Individuals

Copyright ©2015 by Ester R.A. Leutenberg and Carol Butler. All rights reserved. Except for short excerpts for review purposes and materials in the activities and handouts sections, no part of this book may be reproduced or transmitted in any form by any means, electronic or mechanical without permission in writing from the publisher. Activities and handouts are meant to be photocopied.

All efforts have been made to ensure accuracy of the information contained in this book as of the date published. The author(s) and the publisher expressly disclaim responsibility for any adverse effects arising from the use or application of the information contained herein.

Printed in the United States of America

Editorial Director: Carlene Sippola
Art Director: Joy Morgan Dey
Assistant Art Director: Mathew Pawlak

Library of Congress Control Number: 2015942782
ISBN: 978-157025-331-7

Teens ~ Discovering Identity and Moving Toward Independence

The Purpose

Congratulations on taking on the challenges of working with adolescents!

Most teens try on different identities like Halloween costumes.
An image donned may last a day or two, a season, or a lifetime.

This workbook can help teens work on four basic tasks:

- Shed a negative trait, by learning *No trait is cast in stone*.
- See self as clay, molded and remodeled by self as the sculptor.
- Create identities that "fit" today, yet are open to alterations.
- View identities as fluid, not fixed.

Activities in this workbook illuminate the many facets of identity:

- Personal
- Physical
- Emotional
- Cognitive
- Social
- Spiritual
- Independence
- Skills

Through creative expression and interaction, teens are inspired to reach these goals:

- Bring out the best from within.
- Build new strengths.
- Emulate positive role models.
- Reinforce each other's individualism.
- Demonstrate age-appropriate autonomy.
- Develop independent living skills.

May we cherish our teens and uphold this illumination:

*How beautiful is youth!
How bright it gleams with its illusions, aspirations and dreams.*

~ Henry Wadsworth Longfellow

Format of the Book

Introduction for Teen Participants
Present the *Introduction for Teen Participants*, page vii, as an overview before the first activity. This handout is meant to motivate the teens and help them look forward to participating in the activities.

Cover Page for Each Chapter
Each chapter's cover page may be copied and given to teens before the chapter's sessions. This preview provides an inspirational quotation and descriptions to spark interest in the activities. The cover page helps facilitators accomplish the following:
- Stimulate discussion about the quotation.
- Select topics.
- Prepare the group.

After the first activity in each chapter, teens may want to refer to the cover page and vote on which activity to do next.

Unless otherwise stated, there is no particular order for the handouts in the chapters.

Behavioral Coping Skills
The back of each cover page lists the behavioral coping skills in each activity.
- Teens can look forward to skills they will work on and ultimately achieve.
- Facilitators may use these as educational goals and competencies to evaluate.

Chapters
1. Personal Identity
2. Physical Identity
3. Emotional Identity
4. Cognitive Identity
5. Social Identity
6. Spiritual Identity
7. Identity and Independence
8. Daily Skills Matter

Versatility
- One selected chapter may serve as an entire workshop.
- Sessions may be strategically selected to match the skills teens need to develop or enhance.
- Most handouts are adaptable to individual or group use.
- Creative expression, games, puzzles, skits, and other skill-building experiences are provided.

Reproducible Handouts
Facilitators may photocopy and distribute pages as they appear in this workbook, or they may white out and/or add text as desired and then photocopy.

Information on the Back of Each Handout for the Facilitator:
I. **Purpose**
   The goals for the teens in each session.
II. **Skills**
   Behavioral objectives and competencies.
III. **Possible Activities**
   Ways to present topics and responses to elicit.
IV. **Enrichment Activities**
   Additional learning experiences; ways to conclude or follow up.

Skills Teens will Practice in these Chapters

Chapter Skills Pages
Each session's skills are listed on the backs of the chapter cover pages. This list allows teens to preview their expected accomplishments, and facilitators to identify teens' goals and competencies.

Throughout this workbook, teens will be encouraged to engage in the following activities:
Demonstrate oral, written and creative expression skills.
Practice giving and receiving feedback.

Chapter 1. Personal Identity
- Identify and celebrate individual differences.
- Personalize the "different drummer" quote.
- State the futility of comparisons and ways to avoid them.

Chapter 2. Physical Identity
- Articulate gratitude for bodily function.
- Identify physical factors one can or cannot change.
- View self and others with the mind and heart, not just the eyes.
- Document athletic and non-athletic contributions to a team.

Chapter 3. Emotional Identity
- Identify helpful and harmful defense mechanisms.
- Describe ways to feel and deal, rather than numb emotions.
- Demonstrate malleable versus fixed mindsets.
- Create an image for forgiveness and growth.

Chapter 4. Cognitive Identity
- Describe thought changes.
- Note ways to enhance brain function.
- Discuss and debate topics of personal interest.
- Articulate ways to cultivate bravery, strength, and intellect.
- Share about life's lessons learned, and the unknowns.

Chapter 5. Social Identity
- Identify ways to promote positive, and resist negative peer pressure.
- Compare current to future priorities and change activities as warranted.
- Describe potential positive and negative influences of groups.
- Share ways to overcome loneliness.

Chapter 6. Spiritual Identity
- Redirect fear toward positive purposes.
- Compare kite flying facts to self-actualization.
- Create a personal calm in the center of a stormy situation.

Chapter 7. Identity and Independence
- Identify signs of codependency and ways to break the cycle.
- Select an altruistic passion and document an action plan.
- Describe how to choose and be a positive role model.
- Individualize concepts about personal choice, motivation, goals, and challenges.
- Share examples of self-direction versus excessive peer influence.
- Practice negotiation and identify prospective mediators in teen-parent/caregiver conflicts.

Chapter 8. Daily Skills Matter
- Demonstrate examples of progress toward independence regarding: Money, time, career options, employment, safety in several areas of life, physical and emotional health.

Ways to Promote Uniqueness and Age-Appropriate Independence

Sessions
Facilitators can use entire chapters, in the order presented in the book, or choose particular chapters in the order that makes sense for a group's/participant's needs.

If you serve teens with various needs or have time limitations, rather than doing a chapter at a time, consider presenting one handout from each chapter for the first eight sessions; then go back and select another handout from each chapter for subsequent sessions. This method highlights each type of identity and independence and in a condensed time.

Chapters may be presented in any order as a series of workshops.

Gather Materials Before the Session
Most activities require only handouts and pens.
A few facilitator pages suggest optional materials.

Reassure Teens
Participants may volunteer to share or decide not to talk at all.
Remind teens, "What is said in this room stays in this room."
Use code names to protect others' privacy. Example: "MBS" for "My buddy Steve."

Inspire
Encourage teens to stretch slightly beyond their comfort zones when they have the opportunity to lead a team, host a game, act in a skit, express ideas and feelings, and interact with peers.

Spark Interest
Each session begins with a surprising FACT.
A volunteers reads the fact aloud. Encourage peer reactions.

Above all …
Advocate for teens to find their own identity and move forward to their independence.

Motivate teens to appreciate, save, and be able to look back at their work.

Before the first session, ask each teen to bring a three-ring binder with a clear plastic cover. Ask teens to bring current photos and/or other paper memorabilia to create a collage.

During the first session, explain that teens will explore their identities and independence. Ask teens to create a title page, affix photos and mementos, and insert the page under the clear cover.
   Sample title: Me at Age _____. Who I Am Becoming and Where I Am Going.

Throughout this workbook, either use three-hole paper or have a three-hole punch handy. Encourage teens to keep their paperwork in the notebook for future reference.

Introduction for Teen Participants

Teens often wonder "Who am I?"
The answer …
Who do you want to be?

> *Life isn't about finding yourself. Life is about creating yourself.*
> ~ George Bernard Shaw

You are like a sculptor and your identity is a work in process.

You are molding yourself into who you want to be.

Your identity need not harden into a granite or solid steel statue.

You can add, carve out, and re-shape your qualities!

As you chisel your identity, celebrate YOU!

- Your uniqueness
- Your physical being
- Your emotions
- Your thoughts
- Your social life
- Your spirituality
- Your independence
- Your skills

As you bring out your best from within, you will …

- Stand up for your beliefs.
- Respect the rights of others.
- Do more for yourself.
- Pursue your passions.
- Make decisions that will impact the rest of your life
  And the lives of those around you.

**The upcoming activities will help you create yourself,
find your own identity and move toward your independence.**

Teens ~ Discovering Identity and Moving Toward Independence

TABLE OF CONTENTS

1. PERSONAL IDENTITY ...11
Personal Identity Behavioral Coping Skills ...12
- No Two Alike ...13
- What Gets Stuck in Your Head? ...15
- You Decide! ...17
- The Green-Eyed Monster ...19

2. PHYSICAL IDENTITY ...21
Physical Identity Behavioral Coping Skills ...22
- Brain and Body Functions ...23
- Six Aspects of Physical Identity ...25
- See in Every Direction ...27
- Takes Every Able Member ...29
- Your Declaration of Independence ...31

3. EMOTIONAL IDENTITY ...33
Emotional Identity Behavioral Coping Skills ...34
- Defense Mechanisms ...35
- Emotional First Aid: Emotional Pain – Why It Hurts ...37
  - Emotional First Aid: Feel and Deal ...38
  - Emotional First Aid: Ruminate or Re-evaluate? ...39
- Malleable Mindset – Minds Can Change ...41
  - Malleable Mindset – The Process of Trying ...42
  - Malleable Mindset – Labels ...43
- Forgiveness ...45

4. COGNITIVE IDENTITY ...47
Cognitive Identity Behavioral Coping Skills ...48
- My Inner TV ...49
- Brain Development ...51
- Great Debates - Topics ...53
  - Great Debates Talk and Listen ...54
  - Great Debates - Quotations ...55
- Braver, Stronger, Smarter ...57
- I Have Learned ...59

(Continued on the next page)

Teens ~ Discovering Identity and Moving Toward Independence

TABLE OF CONTENTS (continued)

5. SOCIAL IDENTITY 61
   Social Identity Behavioral Coping Skills 62
   - Take Chances with Friends? 63
   - What's in My Cell Phone? 65
   - Social Circles 67
   - I Feel Most Lonely When - Checklist 69
     - I Feel Most Lonely When - Ways to Cope 70
     - When You Feel Most Lonely … - Letter 71

6. SPIRITUAL IDENTITY 73
   Spiritual Identity Behavioral Coping Skills 74
   - Scared? 75
   - Fly like a Kite - Me 77
     - Fly like a Kite - Comparisons 78
     - Fly like a Kite - Connections and Memories 79
   - My Storm - My Situation, Part I 81
     - My Storm - My Situation, Part II 82
     - My Storm - My Calm Place 83

7. IDENTITY AND INDEPENDENCE 85
   Identity and Independence Behavioral Coping Skills 86
   - Codependent? 87
   - Altruism - What's Right In Front of Me? 89
     - Altruism - Connectedness 90
     - Altruism - My Action Plan 91
   - What Influences Teens? - Famous People 93
     - What Influences Teens? - What If? 94
     - What Influences Teens? - Positive Role Models 95
   - "Oh, the Places You'll Go!" 97
   - Autonomy - Diagram 99
     - Autonomy - Diagram Directions 100
     - Autonomy - Advice 101
   - The Art of Negotiation 103

(Continued on the next page)

Teens ~ Discovering Identity and Moving Toward Independence

TABLE OF CONTENTS *(continued)*

8. DAILY SKILLS MATTER 105
Daily Skills Matter Behavioral Coping Skills 106
- Money Matters - Spend, Save, Share 107
    - Money Matters - The ABC's 108
    - Money Matters - My Budget 109
- Time Matters - Pirates 111
    - Time Matters - Interruptions 112
    - Time Matters - Organization 113
- Safety Matters - Street Smarts 115
    - Safety Matters - Home Security 116
    - Safety Matters - Wise on Wheels 117
    - Safety Matters - Privacy 118
    - Safety Matters - Weapons 119
- Job Matters 121
- Career Matters - Choices 123
    - Career Matters - Categories 124
    - Career Matters - Service 125
- Food Matters 127
- Safe Driving Matters 129
- Health Matters 131
- Life Matters 133

Our Deepest Gratitude to
the following professionals who make us look good ...

Illustrator	–	Amy L. Brodsky, LISW-S
Editor and Lifelong Teacher	–	Eileen Regen, M.Ed., CJE
Reviewer / Teen Counselor	–	Niki Tilicki, MAED
Proofreader	–	Jay Leutenberg, CASA
Art Director	–	Joy Dey
Assistant Art Director	–	Mathew Pawlak
Editorial Director	–	Carlene Sippola

PERSONAL IDENTITY 1

The more you like yourself, the less you are like anyone else, which makes you unique.
~ Walt Disney

No Two Alike .... page 13 ▶
Teens celebrate uniqueness using the concept that no two snowflakes are alike. Teens discuss acceptance of similarities and differences among people.

What Gets Stuck in Your Head? .... page 15 ▶
Teens listen to their own heads and hearts using the Thoreau quotation about hearing a different drummer. Teens draw and decorate drums with messages that only they hear, regarding many aspects of their lives.

YOU DECIDE! .... page 17 ▶
Teens recognize the value of individual differences through a game show or individual format. Teens identify ways all individuals and groups can be heard and respected.

The Green-Eyed Monster .... page 19 ▶
Teens explore ways people compare themselves with others. Teens acknowledge the drawbacks of comparisons, ways to avoid them, and the many reasons for individual differences.

Chapter 1 – Personal Identity Skills

Throughout the chapter, teens will communicate through oral, written, and graphic expression, and give and receive feedback.

Teens: Skills in each activity.
Facilitators: Competencies to evaluate.

No Two Alike
- Create a snowflake and acknowledge that all snowflakes differ.
- Identify six or more individual traits.

What Gets Stuck in Your Head?
- Analyze and personalize the Thoreau quotation: *If a man does not keep pace with his companions, perhaps it is because he hears a different drummer. Let him step to music which he hears, however measured or far away.*
- Identify what one likes, dislikes, loves to do, does well, is like inside, hopes to be, and other traits.

You Decide!
- Demonstrate respect for differences in skills, ideas, and interests, in eight situations.
- State eight reasons for choosing individuality versus sameness.

The Green-Eyed Monster
- Identify twelve comparisons as futile.
- Interpret the "apples and oranges" analogy about comparisons.
- Describe a situation in which one compared self to others, the resultant feelings, and reasons why comparisons are senseless.
- State two or more drawbacks of comparisons and four or more ways to avoid them.

Personal Identity

No Two Alike

> **FACT**
> Just like snowflakes, no two people are alike, even identical twins.

Make your own unique snowflake any way you wish or use these suggestions.

1. Fold a piece of paper diagonally to make a triangle.
2. Cut off the rectangular shaped excess paper.
3. Fold the large triangle in half to make a small triangle.
4. Position a point at bottom and fold into thirds:
   (Fold one side toward middle, fold the other side toward the middle; they will overlap.)
5. Cut at an angle below the two points at the top and discard the top.
6. Cut shapes into your remaining triangle's edges – squares, half circles and triangles, etc.
7. Carefully unfold – Voila!! Your original creation.

Write whatever makes *you*, YOU, on your snowflake.

Think about traits related to your:

Actions

Appearance

Feelings

Spirituality

Thoughts

Ways of relating to people

> **There is only 1 you!**

TEENS – DISCOVERING IDENTITY AND MOVING TOWARD INDEPENDENCE

No Two Alike
FOR THE FACILITATOR

I. Purpose
To celebrate uniqueness.

II. Skills
Create a cutout snowflake and acknowledge that all snowflakes differ.
Identify six or more individualistic traits.

III. Possible Activities
   a. Before the session, have plain white paper and scissors available for each teen.
   b. Distribute the *No Two Alike* handout. A volunteer reads the FACT aloud and encourages reactions.
   c. Ask "What's the value of knowing this fact?" (Expect everyone, including yourself, to be different than others).
   d. Direct teens to follow the instructions on the handout.
   e. Allow time for completion.
   f. Encourage teens to show their snowflakes and share traits they are willing to disclose.
   g. Pose the question "Most people either celebrate or try to hide their differences. Why?"
      Elicit that many people try to be like others because they want to fit in.
   h. Ask "What's better than being accepted because of your similarities?"
      Elicit that having unconditional acceptance of similarities and differences is ideal.
   i. Discuss that it is common to conform and imitate. We have to be careful to follow the right example.
   j. Teens may display their snowflakes on a bulletin board.
   k. Prompt teens to brainstorm a title.
      Possibilities
      • Snowflakes and People – No Two Alike
      • What Do Snowflakes and People have in Common?
      • People Are Like Snowflakes – Beautifully Unique

IV. Enrichment Activity
Encourage teens to research celebrities and historical figures with unique characteristics.
Possibilities
   • Some celebrities do not hide the fact that they were born with two different color eyes.
   • Many artists, innovators and world-changers had personalities perceived as "eccentric."

Personal Identity

What Gets Stuck in Your Head?

> **FACT**
> **An earworm is a song that gets stuck in your head.**

What gets stuck in YOUR head?

If a man does not keep pace with his companions, perhaps it is because he hears a different drummer. Let him step to the music which he hears, however measured or far away.

~ Henry David Thoreau

Draw a drum.
Then, decorate your drum with messages only you hear about you and your life.

TEENS – DISCOVERING IDENTITY AND MOVING TOWARD INDEPENDENCE

What Gets Stuck in Your Head?
FOR THE FACILITATOR

I. Purpose
To listen to one's own head and heart.

II. Skills
Analyze and personalize the Thoreau quotation: *If a man does not keep pace with his companions, perhaps it is because he hears a different drummer. Let him step to the music which he hears, however measured or far away.*
Identify what one likes, dislikes, loves to do, does well, is like inside, hopes to be, etc.

III. Possible Activities
   a. Write "Earworm" on the board and ask its meaning (a song that repeats in the mind).
   b. Encourage teens to briefly share tunes and lyrics that get stuck in their heads.
   c. Distribute the *What Gets Stuck in Your Head* handout. A volunteer reads the fact aloud and encourages reactions.
   d. Ask "What does it mean to 'not keep pace' with your companions?"
   (Not keep up or not fit in).
   e. Pose the question "What reason does Thoreau give for not keeping pace?" (A person hears a different drummer).
   f. Ask "Who is the drummer?" (inner-voice, etc.)
   g. Prompt teens to consider the figurative interpretation of drummer.
   (Message, calling, uniqueness).
   h. Encourage teens to interpret "*step to the music … however measured or far away.*"
   (Follow the heart; forge a new path; cultivate interests and talents; let no one diminish one's dreams; a message may be well-thought out or a still small voice).
   i. Direct teens to draw drums and use words, symbols, drawings, and other representations to show what "different drummer" they hear.
   j. If teens need suggestions, encourage them to brainstorm; a volunteer lists their ideas.
   Possibilities
   - What you do well
   - What you love to do
   - What you'd like to do better
   - Who you are inside
   - Who you hope to become
   - Whom/what you are inspired by
   - Your dislikes
   - Your likes
   - Your vision of your adult life
   k. Allow time for completion.
   l. Encourage teens to share their responses and to receive peer feedback.

IV. Enrichment Activities
   a. Tell teens that like musical earworms, put-downs by others or negative self-talk may repeat in their heads, too. A way to get a musical earworm or a negative message out of a person's head is to focus on any puzzle.
   b. Put the following on the board for teens to unscramble.
   "eB uroyesfl; veyrdyboe seel si raelayd ktane." ~ csOar dWlie
   (Answer "Be yourself; everybody else is already taken." ~ Oscar Wilde)

Personal Identity

YOU DECIDE!

> **FACT**
> Decisions: High priced entrees on a menu boosts revenue for the restaurant – even if no one buys them. Why? Because even though people generally won't buy the most expensive dish on the menu, they will order the second most expensive dish.

1. You're opening a restaurant. You can afford to pay three employees. Who will be hired?
   a. Three fabulous chefs.
   b. A public relations person, a chef and an accountant.
   Why?_____

2. You're starting a non-profit to help homeless teens. Who are your three advisors?
   a. A teen who has lived on the streets, a social worker and a fundraiser.
   b. Three professors who wrote an award-winning book about teens living on the streets.
   Why?_____

3. You're starting a website design company. What people do you recruit?
   a. Three creative website designers.
   b. A website designer, a sales person and a bookkeeper.
   Why?_____

4. You're the club president and you are meeting with members about a problem. Which is helpful?
   a. Members all suggest the same solution.
   b. Members debate the pros and cons of different solutions.
   Why?_____

5. You're opening a business in a community flooded by technology companies. You …
   a. Sell popular cell phones.
   b. Provide a service (landscaping, pet walking, etc.).
   Why?_____

6. You're planning a concert to raise funds. How would you sell more tickets?
   a. Recruit musicians who play your best friend's favorite music.
   b. Recruit musicians who play a variety of musical genres.
   Why?_____

7. You're a student surrounded by peers. Which makes more sense?
   a. Be your own person.
   b. Blend in with the others.
   Why?_____

8. Your opinions differ from most people's views. What makes more sense?
   a. Pretend to agree with the majority.
   b. State your opinions respectfully.
   Why?_____

TEENS – DISCOVERING IDENTITY AND MOVING TOWARD INDEPENDENCE

You Decide!

FOR THE FACILITATOR

I. **Purpose**
To recognize the value of individual differences in others and then in oneself.

II. **Skills**
Demonstrate respect for differences in skills, ideas and interests in eight situations.
State eight reasons for choosing individuality versus sameness.

III. **Possible Activities**
  a. Before the session, select either the *Game Show Format* or the *Individual Format*.
  b. Photocopy the *You Decide!* handout as suggested.
  c. At the start of the session tell teens the fact of the day relates to restaurant menus.
  d. Read the FACT from the *You Decide!* handout aloud.
  e. Encourage a brief discussion of favorite eating establishments and factors that affect teens' food choices.

Game Show Format
  - Photocopy one *You Decide!* handout and the *You Decide!* facilitator page.
  - Cut out the Answer Key on this facilitator page and give it to the game show host along with the *You Decide!* handout.
  - Ask for a volunteer game show host, who will read questions aloud.
  - The host will then read each question and two possible responses aloud.
  - The volunteer contestants take turns choosing one response and stating their rationales.
  - After each contestant's turn, the host reveals the preferred response and reason.

Answer Key:

| 1 – b | 2 – a | 3 – b | 4 – b | 5 – b | 6 – b | 7 – a | 8 – b |

Numbers 1 – 6 "Why?" *different abilities, ideas, interests, etc. are needed.*
Number 7 "Why?" *better to be an original than a copy.*
Number 8 "Why?" *better to be authentic and true to oneself.*

Individual Format
  - Photocopy one handout per participant and distribute.
  - Advise teens to circle the letter in front of the best responses and write the reasons.
  - Allow time for completion.
  - Review the Answer Key.

  f. Prompt teens to brainstorm "Who seems to decide who gets heard and respected?" A volunteer lists the group's ideas (parents/caregivers/other adults, cool cliques, the majority, the media, society, politicians, celebrities, etc.).
  g. Ask "In an ideal world who would be heard and respected?" (Every individual, group and/or country).

IV. **Enrichment Activities**
Encourage teens to identify ways all individuals and groups can be heard and respected (share ideas even if other people disagree, listen and consider diverse views, ask questions, write and read editorials and blogs, work together on projects from class assignments to world peace, etc.).

Personal Identity

The Green-Eyed Monster

> **FACT**
> Jealousy is often referred to as "The Green-Eyed Monster,"
> a phrase used by Shakespeare in Othello (Act III).

The surest route to breeding jealousy is to compare. Since jealousy comes from feeling less than another. Comparisons only fan the fire.
~ Dorothy Corkille Briggs

Place an "S" in front of comparisons that make sense.
Place an "F" in front of comparisons that are futile.
(Futile: having no result or effect – pointless or useless)

_____ A blue jay looking at a cardinal decides he is ugly because he is not red.
_____ A fish seeing a squirrel climb a tree feels worthless because he cannot climb.
_____ A rose comparing itself to a daisy hates its own thorns.
_____ A girl staring at a model decides "I'm not pretty or thin enough."
_____ A runner watching a swimmer thinks "I'm no athlete."
_____ A musician admiring an artist's painting infers "I have no talent."
_____ A mechanic needing a plumber says "I'm useless."
_____ A person seeing someone on social media decides "My life is boring."
_____ A math whiz listening to someone speak three languages calls herself "stupid."
_____ A person compares her most disliked trait to a celebrity who had cosmetic surgery.
_____ A healthy athlete compares himself to a person on performance enhancing drugs.
_____ A person preferring solitude feels weird compared to the class president.

The Art Lesson

An art teacher's student developed a cool technique.
A co-worker asked the teacher "Aren't you jealous because the student is so creative?"
The art teacher replied, "No. I don't compare apples and oranges."

What did the teacher mean? _____
_____
_____

Complete the thoughts below

I compared myself with someone when _____
_____
_____

As a result I felt _____
_____
_____

It is senseless to compare myself to others because _____
_____
_____

TEENS – DISCOVERING IDENTITY AND MOVING TOWARD INDEPENDENCE

The Green Eyed Monster
FOR THE FACILITATOR

I. **Purpose**
To acknowledge the futility of comparisons.

II. **Skills**
Identify twelve comparisons as futile.
Interpret the "apples and oranges" analogy about comparisons.
Describe a situation in which one compared oneself with others, list the resultant feelings, and provide reasons comparisons are senseless.
State two or more drawbacks of comparisons and four or more ways to avoid them.

III. **Possible Activities**
   a. Ask a volunteer to draw a monster on the board (with green eyes if a green marker is available).
   b. Distribute The *Green-Eyed Monster* handout.
   c. A volunteer reads the FACT aloud and encourages reactions.
   d. Another teen reads the quotation aloud.
   e. Ask teens to identify ways people compare themselves to others (appearance, money, clothes, cars, grades, abilities, popularity; their photos and portrayals on social media, etc.).
   f. Explain that teens will be thinking about similar comparisons.
   g. Review the directions with teens.
   h. Allow time for completion. Review responses. (All are "futile").
   i. Ask teens the reason the comparisons are futile (two different entities are compared).
   j. Elicit that the art teacher meant that one person's ability cannot be compared with another's because they're different people with unique skills.
   k. Encourage teens to share their sentence starters and receive peer feedback.
   l. Responses will be individualized.
   m. Emphasize the senselessness of comparing oneself with others who have different genetics, environments, interests, abilities and preferences (as in the comparison of a person who prefers solitude to the class president who seeks social settings).

IV. **Enrichment Activities**
   a. Encourage a discussion about the drawbacks of comparisons. (Foster inferiority and envy; people regret what they lack instead of enjoying what they have).
   b. Prompt teens to brainstorm ways to avoid comparisons. (Know "No one else is living my life"; value internal traits of kindness, etc. rather than magnify money, looks, etc. Realize that life is not a contest and that competition has its place in games; do not expect to be perfect or think that someone else has achieved perfection).

PHYSICAL IDENTITY 2

Only when you are aware of the uniqueness of everyone's individual body will you begin to have a sense of your own self-worth.

~ Ma Jian

Brain and Body Functions .... page 23 ▶
Teens acknowledge gratitude for function versus resenting parts of their bodies that do not fit an "ideal" image. Teens discuss the media's role in promoting unrealistic ideals.

Six Aspects of Physical Identity .... page 25 ▶
Teens name six aspects of physical identity and describe their impact. Teens discuss heredity, nutrition, exercise, lifestyle, mind, image, and the interplay between body and mind.

See in Every Direction .... page 27 ▶
Teens demonstrate kindness toward their own physical identities, as opposed to criticism. Teens imagine and draw how their hearts, instead of their eyes, would view their bodies.

Takes Every Able Member .... page 29 ▶
Teens explore ways to contribute to a team, using their particular interests or talents. Teens write athletic and non-athletic role descriptions, and note various endeavors in which their talents can be used.

Your Declaration of Independence .... page 31 ▶
Teens recognize how their physical identities facilitate awareness and appreciation of independence. Teens express creatively what's on their minds and in their hearts about their bodies.

Chapter 2 – Physical Identity Skills

Throughout the chapter, teens will communicate through oral, written, and graphic expression, and give and receive feedback.

Teens: Skills in each activity.
Facilitators: Competencies to evaluate.

Brain and Body Functions
- Identify three or more functions for which to be grateful for each of eight body parts.
- Brainstorm symbolic functions of five or more body parts.

Six Aspects of Physical Identity
- Identify six aspects of physical identity by responding to clues.
- Name five physical factors that can be controlled and one that cannot.
- Describe which factor needs the most change.
- State one or more ways to make the change.
- Brainstorm three or more ways the body and mind affect each other.

See in Every Direction
- Describe five or more ways the heart, rather than eyes, would view one's body.
- Identify five or more ways to view others with one's heart.
- List six or more Do's and Don'ts related to physical identity mindsets.
- Explain the idioms: *the heart of the matter* and *have a heart for ...* related to body image.
- Discuss four or more interpersonal issues related to physical identity.

Takes Every Able Member
- Acknowledge the importance of using unique personal abilities in many different environments.
- Describe one or more ways each of twelve roles can contribute to a football game.
- Identify twelve roles from peers' descriptions.
- State six or more ways non-athletic abilities can be developed and promoted.

Your Declaration of Independence
- Describe ways a unique, strong, physical identity helps teen independence.
- Express thoughts and feelings about physical identity through a journaling and/or art activity.

Physical Identity

Brain and Body Functions

> **FACT**
> When you're awake, your brain generates enough electricity to power a light bulb.

People sometimes dislike something about their face or body that, in their opinion, doesn't compare or measure up to the quality or features of a model, TV or movie star, or someone else they look up to.

It helps to focus on function - on what these features or parts of your body do for you. Below, write about what you are grateful for and why. (Eyes to see a friend's face, ears to hear a favorite song.)

If any part of your body is limited, note how other parts of your body accommodate for that body part.

In each box list at least three functions for which you are grateful.

Eyes	Nose	Mouth	Ears
Stomach	**Brain**	**Arms**	**Legs**
Hands	**Feet**	**Glutes**	**Neck**

TEENS – DISCOVERING IDENTITY AND MOVING TOWARD INDEPENDENCE

Brain and Body Functions

FOR THE FACILITATOR

I. **Purpose**
To acknowledge gratitude for function versus resentment for parts of one's body that do not fit the "ideal" image.

II. **Skills**
Identify three or more functions for which one is grateful for each of eight body parts.

III. **Possible Activities**
a. On the board, write "Fact – When you're awake your brain generates enough electricity to power a light bulb." Encourage reactions.
b. Ask for a show of hands from people who ever complained because their brain didn't ace a test.
c. Encourage a discussion about how the media promotes unrealistic ideals regarding body build, etc.
d. Suggest that people often complain about parts of their body instead of being thankful for the functionality of those body parts.
e. Distribute the *Brain and Body Functions* handout. Ask a volunteer to read the text and instructions aloud.

Game Format
- Divide into teams. Team members sit together to confer.
- Each team is assigned one or more parts of the body and brainstorms responses.
- Each team's secretary lists ideas on the back of the page.
- Teams re-convene and secretaries share their teams' lists.
- Teens return to their seats and write their own responses in all boxes on the front.

Individual Format
- Allow time for completion.
- Encourage teens to share their responses and to receive peer feedback.

Possibilities

Eyes help to see…	Nose helps to …	Mouth helps to …	Ears help to …
Nature's beauty	Breathe and live	Taste favorite food	Learn info for a test
Loved ones faces	Smell pizza	Speak one's truth	Hear a loved one's voice
Body language	Enjoy partner's cologne	Drink when thirsty	Enjoy nature's sounds
Text on a phone	Sense danger (fire)	Comfort with words	Recognize warnings
Stomach helps to …	Brain helps to …	Arms help to …	Legs help to …
Digest food	Figure out solutions	Embrace loved ones	Run to loved ones
Protect internal organs	Feel emotions	Carry gifts	Walk on the beach
Be satisfied after meals	Make decisions	Drive a car	Jump to make a basket
Feel butterflies	React quickly in danger	Shake hands	Walk away when needed
Hands help to …	Feet help to …	Glutes helps to …	Neck helps to …
Touch	Walk	Sit	Hold head up
Write	Run	Keep us upright with	Swallow
Hold	Jog	powerful muscles	Talk
Create	Stand	Cushion our seats	Sing

IV. **Enrichment Activities**
Encourage teens to brainstorm less common and/or symbolic functions of the body.

Possibilities
- Eyes release emotions through tears of joy or sorrow and both are therapeutic.
- A symbolic nose smells a rat, knows when something isn't right.
- People feel in their bones what their brains don't yet know.
- Ears aren't needed to hear the still small voice of truth or faith.
- A gut feeling sometimes serves as a guide.

Six Aspects of Physical Identity

> **FACT**
> The secret behind an efficient honeycomb is due to its hexagonal (six-sided) shape.

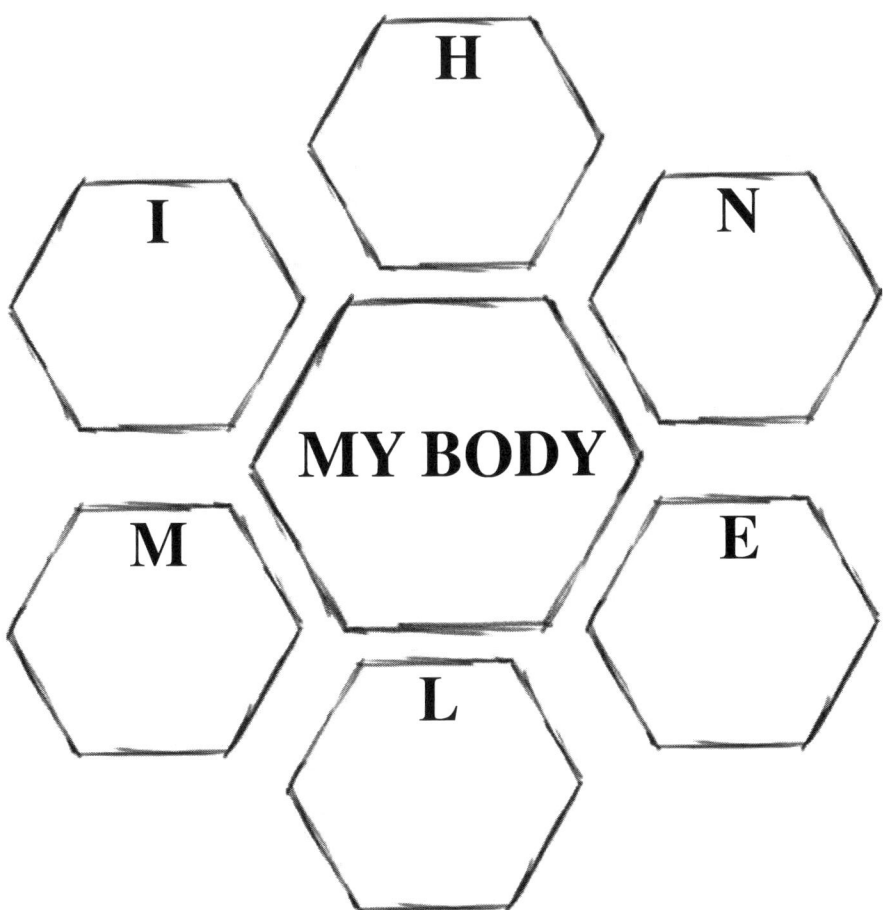

Use the clues below to write a word in each hexagon.

- **H** — Physical and genetic qualities transmitted from one generation to the next
- **N** — A source of materials to nourish the body
- **E** — Exerting muscles to keep fit
- **L** — A way of living that reflects the person's values and attitudes
- **M** — That which is responsible for thoughts and feelings
- **I** — A personal impression presented to the world

How does your lifestyle affect your body? _____

Which one hexagon is not under your control? _____

Which physical trait(s) that cannot be changed do you need to accept? _____

Which hexagon will most benefit from change? _____

What will you do to make the change? _____

TEENS – DISCOVERING IDENTITY AND MOVING TOWARD INDEPENDENCE

Six Aspects of Physical Identity
FOR THE FACILITATOR

I. **Purpose**
   To acknowledge six aspects of physical identity and describe their impact.

II. **Skills**
   List six factors that contribute to physical identity by responding to clues.
   Name five factors that can be controlled and one that cannot.
   Describe which factor needs the most change.
   State one or more ways to make the change.
   Brainstorm three or more ways the body and mind affect each other.

III. **Possible Activities**
   a. Draw a hexagon on the board and ask teens to identify its geometric shape.
   b. Ask "What are six sides of your body?" (Teens may guess front, back, sides, etc.; accept any responses).
   c. Distribute the *Six Aspects of Physical Identity* handout. A volunteer reads the FACT, encourages reactions, and then reads directions aloud.
   d. Allow time for completion.
   e. Encourage teens to share their responses (within their comfort zones) and receive peer feedback.
      Possibilities
      - Hexagon words – **H**eredity, **N**utrition, **E**xercise, **L**ifestyle, **M**ind, and **I**mage.
      - Lifestyle choices (avoid drugs and alcohol, sleep well, etc.) affect appearance and health.
      - Heredity is not under a teen's control.
      - Expect a variety of individualized responses to the last three questions.

IV. **Enrichment Activities**
   a. Write "You are what you think" on the board and ask for interpretations.
   b. Ask teens to brainstorm ways thoughts may affect the body.
      Possibilities
      - Stressful thoughts may lead to headaches, intestinal reactions and other symptoms.
      - Level of self-esteem affects body language (open or closed) and posture (upright or slouched).
      - Thoughts can cause excessive concern about looks or body build or bring peaceful acceptance.
      - Depressing thoughts can lead to disregard for grooming and problems with eating and sleeping.
   c. Ask teens to identify ways the body may affect the mind.
      Possibilities
      - Chemical imbalances may lead to unwanted thoughts, feelings, perceptions (hearing voices, etc.).
      - Severe or chronic pain can cause anxious or sad thoughts.
      - Many physical conditions can affect the mind and body (fluctuations in blood sugar, etc.)

Physical Identity

See in Every Direction

> **FACT**
> Bees have five eyes and can easily see movement in any direction. Bees don't see as well when everything holds still, which is why holding still can often prevent bee stings.

Draw your face with big hearts for eyes.
Write in the hearts how you would view your body with your heart instead of your eyes.
   (Example – appreciation instead of criticism.)

How would you see _____ if you followed this suggestion?
   (A PERSON IN YOUR LIFE – USE A NAME CODE)

Look with your heart and not with your eyes.
~ *Andrew Lloyd Webber*

_____
_____
_____

TEENS – DISCOVERING IDENTITY AND MOVING TOWARD INDEPENDENCE

See in Every Direction
FOR THE FACILITATOR

I. Purpose
To demonstrate kindness toward one's physical identity as opposed to criticism.

II. Skills
Describe five or more ways one's heart, rather than eyes, would view one's body.
Identify five or more ways to view others with one's heart.
List six or more Physical Identity Mindsets *Do's and Don'ts*

III. Possible Activities
a. Ask a volunteer to draw a big heart on the board.
b. Encourage a discussion of the heart's symbolism (the center of emotion, affection, love, caring).
c. Distribute the *See in Every Direction* handout. A volunteer reads the FACT, encourages reactions, and reads the directions below the box aloud.
d. Allow time for completion.
e. Encourage teens to share their responses and receive to peer feedback.
   Possibilities
   Ways the heart might view the body – with love, acceptance, nurturance, compassion, amazement at its complexity and joy in its pleasures.
   Look with your heart…Discover people's interests, abilities, needs, struggles, etc. Find ways to show respect and help others.
f. Encourage teens to brainstorm Physical Identity Mindsets *Do's* and *Don'ts*. This may be done as a board activity or in teams or individually.
   Possibilities

Physical Identity Mindsets - Don't	Physical Identity Mindsets - Do
Hate it.	Embrace it; nobody (*no body*) is perfect.
Compare it with others.	Nurture it with a healthy food routine.
Starve it.	Enjoy it with a regular exercise program.
Over-feed it.	Love its natural shape.
Beat it into shape with strenuous workouts.	Comfort it with hot showers, etc.
Force it to be something it's not.	Celebrate its abilities.
Expect it to be perfect.	Treat it as a best friend.
Tell it what it's *not*.	Thank it for *X* number of years of service.

IV. Enrichment Activities
a. Write the italicized idioms on the board; ask teens to relate them to body image.
   The heart of the matter
      Elicit that the central issue of dissatisfaction with the body is usually something else – the influence of critical family or friends, unrealistic media images, other issues in one's life (low self-esteem, power struggles, emotional issues, etc.)
   Have a heart for …
      Elicit that to have compassion and to focus energy on social, political or environmental causes, will minimize dwelling on one's body image, diet, competition, etc.
b. Encourage a discussion about interpersonal issues related to physical identity.
   Possibilities
   - Seek friends who value inner traits rather than superficial appearance-related assets.
   - Talk with people about topics other than diet, exercise, athletic abilities and clothes.
   - Find healthy activities to do with people – hiking, dancing and sports.
   - Perform acts of kindness with peers – sing at a children's hospital or a facility for people who are elderly – to reinforce inner-traits of compassion, etc.

Physical Identity ▶

Takes Every Able Member

> **FACT**
> The mere presence of other people, either engaged in the same task or having the same passion, can boost motivation.

In the T.E.A.M., all abilities are equally important.
Cut out each role below. On the back of each role write how that particular person can use his/her abilities to contribute to a football team.
You may later volunteer to have your cutouts used in a game.

The T.E.A.M.

Sports Star	Team Player	Coach	Math Whiz
Writer	Artist	Advertiser	Fan
Fund Raiser	Stadium Manager	Food Vendor	Musician

© 2015 WHOLE PERSON ASSOCIATES, 101 W. 2ND ST., SUITE 203, DULUTH MN 55802 • 800-247-6789

TEENS – DISCOVERING IDENTITY AND MOVING TOWARD INDEPENDENCE

Takes Every Able Member
FOR THE FACILITATOR

I. Purpose
To illustrate that people can be integral parts of many different endeavors, using their particular interests or talents.

II. Skills
Acknowledge the importance of using one's unique abilities in many different environments.
Describe one or more ways that each of twelve roles can contribute to a football game.
Identify twelve roles from peers' *T.E.A.M.* descriptions.
State six or more ways non-athletic abilities can be developed and promoted.

III. Possible Activities
a. Distribute the *Takes Every Able Member* handout. Ask a teen to read the FACT aloud and encourage reactions.
b. Direct teens to cut out the twelve roles and write on the backs how they can use their abilities.
c. Ask for a volunteer to submit a set of cutouts to be used in the first round.
d. In each turn, teens will do the following:
   - Pick up a cutout.
   - Read the *description* on the back or make up their own description.
   - Call on volunteers to guess the *role*.
e. Continue playing until all twelve roles have been described.
f. Another round may be played with a different teen's set of cutouts.

Possibilities for how each team member can use their ability with a football team.
- Sports Star – score many points
- Team player – play one's best
- Coach – teach and guide
- Math Whiz – figure angles, velocities, odds, etc., and manage the team's budget
- Writer – compose human interest articles about the players
- Artist – illustrate the action
- Advertiser – promote the games through multiple media venues
- Fan – cheer whether the team is winning or losing
- Fundraiser – create money-making opportunities
- Stadium manager – provide a safe and secure environment
- Food Vendor – serve delicious, healthy and affordable snacks
- Musicians – play theme music in a marching band

IV. Enrichment Activities
Encourage teens to identify activities in which skills other than athletics can be highlighted (trivia bowls, school and community theater and concerts, poetry slams, pet shows, charitable events, etc.).

Physical Identity

Your Declaration of Independence

> **FACT**
> After Thomas Jefferson wrote his first draft of the Declaration, the other members of the Declaration Committee and the Continental Congress made 86 changes to Jefferson's draft, including shortening the overall length by more than a half.

Journal how appreciating your own unique, strong, physical identity can help you to be independent, think for yourself, and express what's on your mind, and in your heart and soul. JUST START WRITING. Similar to Jefferson and his committee, you can go back later and make changes. You may add or delete anything you wish.

_____
_____
_____
_____
_____
_____
_____
_____
_____
_____
_____
_____
_____
_____
_____
_____
_____
_____
_____
_____
_____
_____
_____
_____
_____

TEENS – DISCOVERING IDENTITY AND MOVING TOWARD INDEPENDENCE

Your Declaration of Independence
FOR THE FACILITATOR

I. Purpose
To recognize how awareness and appreciation of one's physical identity facilitates independence.

II. Skills
Describe how a unique, strong, physical identity promotes independence when one is pressured to conform through a written or creative graphic expression.

III. Possible Activities
a. Remind teens that in prior sessions they worked to define and accept their physical identities.
b. Distribute the *Your Declaration of Independence* handout. Ask a volunteer to read the FACT, encourage reactions, and then read directions aloud.
c. Emphasize that ideas and feelings, not grammar and spelling, are important for this journaling exercise.
d. Allow time for completion.
e. If teens wish, encourage them to share their responses and receive peer feedback. Expect a variety of essays from teens who choose to declare their independence in their own way.

IV. Enrichment Activities
An enrichment activity for all or alternate activity for teens who prefer creative graphic expression:
a. Have poster paper and color markers available, or teens may use the backs of the handouts and pens.
b. Write the following quotation on the board.*
"He who works with his hands and his head and his heart is an artist."
Ask a volunteer to read it aloud.
c. Emphasize that talent is not required for this creative graphic expression exercise. They may use sketches, cartoons, collages, symbols, pictures from magazines, etc., to convey their ideas.
d. Prompt teens to use their creative hands to show how a unique, strong, physical identity promotes their independence.
e. Allow time for completion. Encourage teens to share their pictures and receive peer feedback.

---

* This quotation has been attributed to St. Francis of Assisi and to Louis Nizer; some claim that neither man originated the quote and its true source is unknown.

EMOTIONAL IDENTITY 3

Comfort in expressing your emotions will allow you to share the best of yourself with others, but not being able to control your emotions will reveal your worst.
~ Bryant H. McGill

Defense Mechanisms .... page 35 ▶
Teens recognize defense mechanisms, minimize the use of harmful ones and maximize the use of helpful ones. Teens describe examples of fourteen defense mechanisms through the written word and skits.

Emotional First Aid .... page 37 ▶
Teens acknowledge factors related to emotional pain and productive ways to cope. Teens compose six-word slogans for bumper stickers or bulletin boards.

Malleable Mindset .... page 41 ▶
Teens learn to adopt a mindset that promotes actions to develop positive traits and change negative traits. Teens describe labels that others place on them, labels they place on others, and labels they place on themselves.

Forgiveness .... page 45 ▶
Teens acknowledge ways that forgiving others facilitates personal healing and moving forward. Teens share how they have felt when they were forgiven.

Chapter 3 – Emotional Identity Skills

Throughout the chapter, teens will communicate through oral, written, and graphic expression, and give and receive feedback.

Teens: Skills in each activity.
Facilitators: Competencies to evaluate.

Defense Mechanisms
- Give an example of fourteen defense mechanisms.
- Differentiate between the defense mechanisms that are usually harmful and those that are usually helpful.
- Rank order the three defense mechanisms the teen uses most often.
- Discuss three or more defense mechanisms that can be helpful or harmful depending on degree and circumstance.

Emotional First Aid
- Identify four causes of emotional pain.
- Compare physical and emotional pain in terms of their reality and value.
- Acknowledge that to numb emotional pain may worsen it, and numbing does not always solve problems.
- Categorize twenty-three reactions into three categories – *Numb, Feel, and Deal*.
- Differentiate between healthy expressions and negative ruminations that worsen pain.
- Describe a difficult situation, and then explain how one would ruminate, re-evaluate, and act toward desired outcome.
- Compose a six-word slogan about dealing with emotions.

Malleable Mindset
- Describe three traits to change and the accompanying new belief, the first action and the mindset.
- Match four positive traits with the *Process of Trying* action that develops each trait.
- Match seven negative traits with the *Process of Trying* action that changes each trait.
- Write a label placed on self by others, a label placed on others by self, and a label placed on self by self.
- Refute three or more labels with *Process of Trying* statements to develop positive traits and change negative traits.

Forgiveness
Contrast being toxic or unforgiving with the antidote of forgiving by using some of the following actions:
- Create an image for resentment and refusal.
- Create an image for healing and moving forward.
- Differentiate between seven unforgiving attitudes and seven forgiving attitudes by selecting the correct terms.
- Discuss four concepts about forgiving.
- Complete two or more sentence starters about not forgiving and forgiving.
- Share personal experiences with forgiving and being forgiven after reading two pertinent quotations.
- Discuss the concept of forgiving, not forgetting, thus learning from the experience.

Emotional Identity ▶

DEFENSE MECHANISMS

> **FACT**
> *Playing possum* means playing dead. The American opossum, found from Canada to Costa Rica, usually reacts to danger as many mammals do, by hissing, growling, and baring its teeth. However, if this all fails, Plan B is to feign death. The opossum collapses to the ground, drools as if it were ill, and it then remains motionless.

To run away from danger is self-defense. To *run from* reality is a defense mechanism.

For each defense mechanism definition on the left, write an example on the right.
Place a minus (-) in definition boxes you think are usually harmful.
Place a plus (+) in definition boxes those you think are usually helpful.
In the margin next to the definitions, rank order #1, #2, and #3 to show those you use most often.

Definitions of Defense Mechanisms	Examples of Defense Mechanisms
Example: *Compartmentalize* *Have different values at different times*	**Example:** *I am honest and never steal from a store. I did cheat on an exam but "that's different."*
Compartmentalize Segregate parts of self that have different values	
Regress Go back an earlier, more childish stage	
Dissociate Lose sense of time	
Deny Fail to accept a painful reality	
Project Accuse others of one's own thoughts	
Repress Block out memories	
Displace Take out anger on an innocent person	
Rationalize Justify to avoid the truth	
Sublimate Change an impulse into productive action	
Compensate Make up for a real or imaginary weakness	
Assert Express oneself in an honest, open and direct way	
Identify with an aggressor Take the side of, or act like, an abuser	
Avoid Stay away from disliked situations/people	
Humor Use jokes/laughter to cover uncomfortable feelings	

TEENS – DISCOVERING IDENTITY AND MOVING TOWARD INDEPENDENCE

Defense Mechanisms
FOR THE FACILITATOR

I. Purpose
To recognize defense mechanisms, minimize use of harmful ones and maximize use of helpful ones.

II. Skills
Give an example of fourteen defense mechanisms.
Differentiate between those that are usually harmful and those that are usually helpful.
Rank order the three defense mechanisms one uses most often.
Discuss three or more mechanisms that can be helpful or harmful depending on degree and circumstance.

III. Possible Activities
a. Ask teens what they know about self-defense (locks, alarm systems, martial arts, pepper spray, etc.).
b. Distribute the *Defense Mechanisms* handout. Ask a volunteer to read the FACT aloud, encourage reactions, and then read the directions.
c. If teens request help, share one of the examples below under III. e – Possibilities.
d. Allow time for completion.
e. Encourage teens to share their responses and to receive peer feedback.
   Possibilities

Examples of Defense Mechanisms	Examples of Defense Mechanisms
Compartmentalize – generous with money but not love	**Rationalize** – "I drink due to school stress"
Regress – cling to a stuffed toy	**Sublimate** – feel anger, take boxing lessons
Dissociate – "Who am I? Where am I?"	**Compensate** – "I can't sing but I can dance"
Deny – "I don't have a drug problem."	**Assert** – "No … I feel … Please …"
Project – steal and call everyone else "thieves"	**Identify with aggressor** – cling, copy abuser
Repress – "I have no memory of abuse"	**Avoid** – stay in bed on final exam day
Displace – angry at partner and kick the cat	**Humor** – snicker when sex is mentioned

   • Most are harmful (-); the helpful (+) mechanisms are sublimation, compensation and assertiveness.
   • Rank orders will be individualized.
f. Ask teens "Which mechanisms can be harmful or helpful depending on the degree and circumstance?"
   Possibilities
   • Identification with the aggressor can save the life of a hostage but can hurt if continued after release.
   • Humor can relieve tension; it helps to see the funny side of a difficulty.
   • Avoidance of temptation or toxic situations can help; handling toxic situations with coping skills may be more helpful.

IV. Enrichment Activities
Suggest mock videos in which teens individually or in groups present skits that illustrate harmful and helpful defense mechanisms. Ask the audience members to guess the defense mechanisms being portrayed.

Emotional First Aid: Emotional Pain – Why It Hurts

FACT
The same areas of the brain are activated when we experience rejection as when we feel physical pain. That's why it hurts so much!

**Draw a cracked line to show a broken heart.
Label each arrow with a possible cause of emotional pain.**

TEENS – DISCOVERING IDENTITY AND MOVING TOWARD INDEPENDENCE

Emotional First Aid: Feel and Deal

> **FACT**
> "Numbing the pain for a while will only make it worse when you finally feel it."
> ~ J. K. Rowling

Why is physical pain helpful? _____
_____
_____

Why is emotional pain helpful? _____
_____
_____

Place the number for each technique on the step below that describes it.

1. Drink or use drugs
2. Talk about it
3. Binge on anything
4. Re-play it in your mind
5. Journal about it
6. Write a poem about it
7. Learn from it
8. See it differently
9. Put yourself down
10. Problem-solve
11. Forgive self and others
12. Make amends if needed
13. Do something worthwhile
14. Post it on social media
15. Help people in similar situations
16. Fear consequences
17. Try to prevent others from experiencing it
18. Seek spiritual counseling or discover strength from within
19. Research solutions
20. Pretend it never happened
21. Identify positive aspects of the situation
22. Control your time and priorities
23. Have hope
24. Be grateful
25. Use a support system
26. Improve habits
27. Keep life or death secrets
28. Suicide
29. Harm self
30. Hurt others

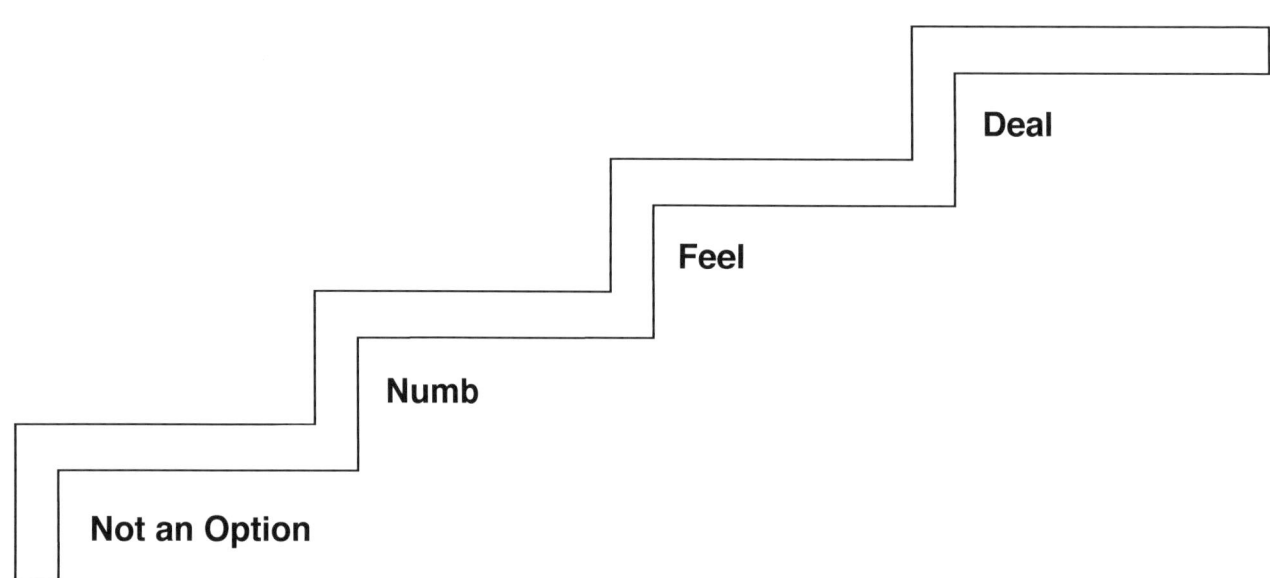

Deal

Feel

Numb

Not an Option

Emotional Identity

Emotional First Aid: Ruminate or Re-evaluate?

> **FACT**
> The word "ruminate" derives from the Latin for chewing cud, in which cattle grind up, swallow, then regurgitate and re-chew their feed. Similarly, human ruminators dwell on an issue at length.

To **ruminate** is to mentally replay negative situations over and over, focusing on problems, but not solutions.
Example: a person is turned down for a date and spends days re-living it and saying "I'm a loser."

To **re-evaluate** is to re-appraise the situation from a positive or possibility point of view.
Example: a person turned down for a date decides "I'll find someone I like who likes me."

To **act** is to take steps toward the desired outcome.
Example: a person turned down for a date joins a club to meet people with similar interests.

Share your real or imaginary negative situation and how you could react in different ways.

My difficult situation ...

_____
_____
_____

If I choose to ruminate I could ...

_____
_____
_____

If I choose to re-evaluate I could ...

_____
_____
_____

If I choose to act I could ...

_____
_____
_____

TEENS – DISCOVERING IDENTITY AND MOVING TOWARD INDEPENDENCE

Emotional First Aid

FOR THE FACILITATOR

I. Purpose
To acknowledge factors related to emotional pain and productive ways to cope.

II. Skills
Identify four causes of emotional pain.
Compare physical and emotional pain in terms of their reality and value.
Acknowledge that to numb emotional pain may worsen it. Numbing does not solve problems.
Categorize thirty reactions into four categories – Not an Option, Numb, Feel, and Deal.
Differentiate between healthy expression and negative ruminations that worsen pain.
Describe a difficult situation and how one could ruminate, re-evaluate and act toward the desired outcome.
Compose a six-word slogan about dealing with emotions.

III. Possible Activities
  a. Plan to present each page in order, during the same or consecutive sessions.
      Emotional First Aid: Emotional Pain – Why It Hurts, *Page* 37
      Emotional First Aid: Feel and Deal, *Page* 38
      Emotional First Aid: Ruminate or Re-evaluate?, *Page* 39
  b. Introduce the first session by asking "What's the first aid for a scraped knee?" (Cleanse and bandage).
  c. Pose the question "What is emotional first aid?" (To recognize emotional injuries, help them heal, etc.).
   Format for each page
   - Distribute the handout. Ask a volunteer to read the FACT aloud and encourage reactions.
   - Allow time for completion.
   - Encourage teens to share responses and to receive peer feedback.
   Possibilities
   Emotional First Aid: Emotional Pain – Why It Hurts, *Page* 37 responses
       Causes may be perceived failure, rejection, guilt, grief, loneliness, anger, resentment, envy, etc.
   Emotional First Aid: Feel and Deal, *Page* 38 responses
   - Physical pain is helpful because it warns us that our bodies need help and/or medical attention.
   - Emotional pain helps us recognize that our thoughts, feelings and/or actions need help and/or change.

| Not an Option | Numb | Feel | Deal 7, 8, 10, 11, 12, 13, 15, 17, |
| 27, 28, 29, 30 | 1, 3, 20 | 2, 4, 5, 6, 9, 14, 16 | 18, 19, 21, 22, 23, 24, 25, 26 |

   Concepts to elicit
       In some cases to *feel* through healthy expression (talk, journal, draw, or write a poem) can be a way to *deal*; ideally the talking, drawing, or writing will lead to insights and solutions.
   Additional activity
       Ask teens which of the *feel* methods worsen pain – 4, 9, 14, 16
   Emotional First Aid: Ruminate or Re-evaluate?, *Page* 39 responses
   - Responses will be individualized.
   - Facilitators know that ideally teens will use a real situation they face; the "imaginary" option is available for teens do not want to admit a problem is real or prefer to use their imaginations.

IV. Enrichment Activities
  a. Encourage teens to compose six-word slogans, individually or in teams.
      Example "I feel, I deal, I heal."
  b. Encourage teens to share their slogans and/or make bulletin board posters, bumper stickers, etc.

Emotional Identity

Malleable Mindset – Minds Can Change

> **FACT**
> Gold is the most malleable (capable of being stretched or bent into different shapes) metal. One ounce of gold can be hammered into a 300 square foot sheet.

A FIXED mindset is the belief that you CAN'T change.
Example: Trait: Outgoing or shy.
Fixed Belief: I'm shy.
Fixed Action: Talk to no one at lunch.
Fixed Mindset: I will always be shy.

A MALLEABLE mindset is the belief that you CAN change.
Example: Trait I Can Change: Outgoing or shy.
Malleable Belief: I can act outgoing.
Malleable First Action: Talk to one person every day at lunch.
Malleable Mindset: I am becoming more outgoing.

My *malleable* mindset is the belief that I can change.

My Trait I Can Change _____

My Malleable Belief _____

My Malleable First Action _____

My Malleable Mindset: _____

My *malleable* mindset is the belief that I can change.

My Trait I Can Change _____

My Malleable Belief _____

My Malleable First Action _____

My Malleable Mindset: _____

My *malleable* mindset is the belief that I can change.

My Trait I Can Change _____

My Malleable Belief _____

My Malleable First Action _____

My Malleable Mindset: _____

TEENS – DISCOVERING IDENTITY AND MOVING TOWARD INDEPENDENCE

Malleable Mindset – The Process of Trying

> **FACT**
> Studies showed that students praised for intelligence avoided tasks they would have to work at because they wanted to uphold their image.
> They feared if they failed it would mean they were not smart.
> Students praised for the process of trying saw challenges as opportunities to learn.

Positive traits are not fixed (forever) because they can develop or decline.

Next to each trait write the letter(s) for the process that helps it develop.

Positive Traits	The Process of Trying to Develop the Trait.
Smart	A. Practicing daily
Well-liked	B. Saving, spending and giving to charity
Rich	C. Trying many strategies to see which works
Talented Musician	D. Being friendly toward many people

Negative traits are not *fixed* (unmoving) because they can be *fixed* (changed)!

Next to each trait write the letter(s) for its *fix*.

Negative Traits	The Process of Trying to Change the Trait
Afraid	A. Developing individual interests
Cheater	B. Participating in a recovery program
Clingy	C. Thinking before speaking
Uncaring	D. Concentrating to improve focus
Addict	E. Doing own homework
Big Mouth	F. Doing random acts of kindness
Distractible	G. Accepting challenges

Emotional Identity

Malleable Mindset – Labels

> **FACT**
> The labels on apples are made of edible paper and edible glue.
> It's still best to peel them off. The easiest way is with scotch tape.

A label is a brief description for purposes of identification.

What do you think is a difference between a label on food and a label on a person?

_____

_____

Write a word or phrase that describes a label someone else has placed on you.

Write a word or phrase that describes a label you placed on someone else.

Write a word or phrase that describes a label you have placed on yourself.

TEENS – DISCOVERING IDENTITY AND MOVING TOWARD INDEPENDENCE

Malleable Mindset
FOR THE FACILITATOR

I. Purpose
To adopt a mindset that promotes actions to develop positive traits and actions to change negative traits.

II. Skills
Describe three traits to change and the accompanying new belief, first action and mindset.
Match four positive traits with the *Process of Trying* action that develops each trait.
Match seven negative traits with the *Process of Trying* action that changes each trait.
Write a label placed on self by others, a label placed on others by self, a label placed on self by self.
Refute three or more labels with *Process of Trying* statements to develop positive/change negative traits.

III. Possible Activities
a. Plan to present each page in order, one at a time, during the same or consecutive sessions.
b. Before the first session, ask teens what they know about gold (expensive, beautiful).
c. Distribute the **Malleable Mindset - Minds Can Change** handout, page 41.
   A volunteer reads the FACT aloud, encourages reactions, and then reads the examples aloud.
   Allow time for completion, encourage teens to share responses and to receive peer feedback.
d. Distribute the **Malleable Mindset - The Process of Trying** handout, page 42.
   A volunteer reads the FACT aloud, encourages reactions and then reads the directions aloud.
   Allow time for completion, encourage teens to share responses and to receive peer feedback.
   Answer Key Suggestions. (Additional letters may be used).
   Positive Traits – C, D, B, A; Negative Traits – G, E, A, F, B, C, D
e. Distribute the **Malleable Mindset - Labels** handout, page 43.
   A volunteer reads the FACT aloud, encourages reactions and then reads the definition aloud.
   Discuss responses to the question at the top of the page (a label on a person hurts and sticks!).
   Ask teens to avoid putting any names on their labels; allow time for writing on the labels.
   Encourage teens to write some positive and some negative labels.
   Direct teens to cut out their labels or fold/tear the page into three parts.
   Tell teens they may enter their labels into a game if they wish.
   - Teens submit their labels for the game.
   - Facilitators silently read labels and set aside any that would identify someone in the group.
   - Players take turns reading a label aloud and eliciting *process of trying* responses from peers.
   Possibilities
   - Lazy – "I'm accomplishing items on a *Things-to-Do* list."
   - Bully – "I'm treating people as I want to be treated."
   - Liar – "I'm admitting my mistakes."
   - Snitch – "I'm telling secrets only if someone's life or safety are involved."
   - Well-Dressed – "I'm wearing styles that make me look good."
   - Healthy – "I'm exercising daily."

IV. Enrichment Activities
Encourage a discussion about labels on merchandise.
- How important are designer labels on clothes and accessories? (Individualized responses)
- Why are labels important to some people? (They like the style or to impress others).
- Encourage teams or individuals to research their favorite brands to determine whether child labor, sweatshops or other unethical practices are involved in their manufacture.

Emotional Identity

Forgiveness

> **FACT**
> Fifty words can be found in the word FORGIVE.
> How many words can you find?

Being "TOXIC" is acting as, or having the effect of, a poison.
An "ANTIDOTE" is a remedy to counteract the effects of a toxin.

UNFORGIVING = TOXIC	**FORGIVING = THE ANTIDOTE**
To be full of resentment and refusing to forgive.	To forgive is healing and moving forward.
Create an image for resentment and refusal.	*Create an image for healing and moving forward.*

Use terms from words below to fill in the blanks.

blame . victim . anger . deserve . myself . worst . power

IF I AM UNFORGIVING …

I give my _____ to the person.

I hurt _____ more than the offender.

I allow myself to remain a _____.

The person does not _____ to be forgiven.

I expect the _____ from everyone.

I _____ others and/or myself.

Misery and _____ take up space in my head.

Use terms from words below to fill in the blanks.

thankful . deserve . love . power . hope . myself . thrive

IF I FORGIVE …

I reclaim my _____ to heal.

I forgive to help _____.

I survive and _____ (rhymes with survive).

I _____ freedom from the poison of the past.

I have _____ for humanity.

I am _____ for lessons learned.

I free up space in my head for health and _____.

To forgive does *not* mean to forget. It allows one to learn and grow from the experience.
To forgive does *not* mean to tolerate continued abuse.
Forgiveness involves responsibility for your own emotional and physical safety.
Forgiveness is part of moving forward in life but it is not the only intervention.
It may help to talk with a trusted adult, a mental health or faith-based counselor.

TEENS – DISCOVERING IDENTITY AND MOVING TOWARD INDEPENDENCE

Forgiveness
FOR THE FACILITATOR

I. Purpose
To forgive in order to facilitate personal healing and moving forward.

II. Skills
Contrast being toxic or unforgiving with the antidote of forgiving by discussing the following steps:
- Create an image for resentment and refusal.
- Create an image for healing and moving forward.
- Differentiate between seven unforgiving and seven forgiving attitudes by selecting the correct terms.
- Discuss four concepts about forgiving.
- Complete two or more sentence starters about not forgiving and forgiving.
- Share personal experiences with forgiving and being forgiven after reading two pertinent quotations.

III. Possible Activities
a. Ask teens what to do if someone is poisoned (go to an emergency room where they may give a medicine to counteract the poison, induce vomiting, etc.).
b. Distribute the *Forgiveness* handout. A volunteer reads the FACT, encourages reactions, and then reads the definitions and directions aloud.
c. Ask teens to create the images through sketches, symbols, cartoons; they may add words.
d. Remind teens that ideas, not artistic ability, are needed for this activity.
e. Allow time for completion.
f. Encourage teens to share their images and to receive peer feedback.
   Possibilities
   Skull and Crossbones, or a bottle of poison, for UNFORGIVING = TOXIC.
   Hands clasped, thumbs up, or a handshake for FORGIVING = THE ANTIDOTE.
   Answer key
   - UNFORGIVING – power, myself, victim, deserve, worst, blame, anger.
   - FORGIVING – power, myself, thrive, deserve, hope, thankful, love.
g. Encourage teens to share experiences related to the five concepts below the boxes.

IV. Enrichment Activities
a. Direct teams or individuals to write endings to these sentences starters as many times as possible in ten minutes:
   Not forgiving is like … (getting your own hands filthy throwing dirt at someone else).
   Forgiving is like … (clearing your head for creativity).
   Encourage teams or individuals to share their responses and receive peer feedback.
b. Write the following quotation on the board.
   To forgive is to set a prisoner free and discover that the prisoner was you. ~ Lewis B. Smedes
   Encourage teens to share how they have been set free by forgiving.
c. Write the following quotation on the board.
   Nothing enables us to forgive like knowing in our hearts that we have been forgiven. ~ Lewis B. Smedes
   Suggest that teens share how they felt when they received the gift of being forgiven.
d. Re: FACT - the 50 words that can be made from the letters in forgive are:
   fiver, forge, giver, gofer, grief, grove, ogive, vigor, vireo, ergo, fire, five, fore, frig, froe, frog, giro, give, goer, gore, ogre, over, rife, rive, rove, vier, ego, erg, fie, fig, fir, foe, fog, for, fro, ire, ore, ref, rei, rev, rig, roe, veg, vie, er, go, if, of, or, re.
   Ask which of those words might pertain to forgiveness. *(ego, over, if, giver, ire)*

COGNITIVE IDENTITY 4

As a single footstep will not make a path on the earth, so a single thought will not make a pathway in the mind. To make a deep physical path, we walk again and again. To make a deep mental path, we must think over and over the kind of thoughts we want to dominate our lives.

~ Henry David Thoreau

My Inner TV .... page 49 ▶
Teens compare their thoughts to a television screen and depict and/or describe positive personal programs. Teens describe ways a TV remote resembles ways they can control their own thoughts.

Brain Development .... page 51 ▶
Teens describe ways to develop the brain's abilities to organize, build skills, apply brakes, and plan. Teens identify ways to promote brain health and prevent detrimental activities that could harm brain function.

Great Debates .... page 53 ▶
Teens develop a cognitive identity as persons who think, speak, listen to others, and substantiate their own opinions through the process of debating. Teens interpret the five C's of 21st century skills.

Braver, Stronger, and Smarter .... page 57 ▶
Teens use thoughts to promote positive actions. Teens personalize an A.A. Milne quotation by identifying everyday ways to act brave, strong, and smart.

I Have Learned .... page 59 ▶
Teens think about life's lessons learned to date, share wisdom with peers, and look toward the future. Teens participate in an "It Remains Unknown" paper pass or a brainstorming session.

Chapter 4 – Cognitive Identity Skills

Throughout the chapter, teens will communicate through oral, written, and graphic expression, and give and receive feedback.

Teens: Skills in each activity.
Facilitators: Competencies to evaluate.

My Inner TV
- Verbalize three or more ways the ability to control personal thoughts resembles a TV remote control.
- Personalize a quotation that uses a TV analogy.
- Explain the power of thoughts.
- Create what one wants to believe, see, hear, and replay about self.
- Practice positive visualization about an upcoming challenge – focus on behavior, not outcomes.
- Identify eight or more types of remote controls.
- Identify four or more ways that remote controls relate to types of thoughts.

Brain Development
- Identify three or more ways to enhance the brain's ability to do the following:
    - Organize thoughts
    - Develop skills
    - Control impulses
    - Plan ahead
- State three ways to promote brain health.
- State three actions that can harm the brain.
- Discuss seven or more effects of sleep deprivation on the brain.
- Research and report about seven or more effects of alcohol on the teen brain.

Great Debates
- Select a topic of interest from among twenty options.
- State whether one is Pro or Con, and the reasons.
- Document an opponent's views.
- Rebut the opposing opinions.
- Discuss benefits of the *Five C's of 21st Century Skills*.

Braver, Stronger, Smarter
- Acknowledge the importance of thoughts and actions in establishing connections in the brain.
- Identify five or more everyday ways to act brave, strong, and smart.
- State actions that can result from beliefs in one's own bravery, strength, and intellect.
- Share personal actions being taken to cultivate different types of bravery, strength, and intellect.
- Imagine other ways to exemplify positive traits through actions.

I Have Learned
- Identify three concepts learned in life.
- Describe one or more things hoped to learn about life in the future.
- Share knowledge and questions about life with peers.

Cognitive Identity

My Inner TV

> **FACT**
> In the teen brain, new interests cause new connections to grow.
> Unused connections die away.
> Nerve cells grow thick coats of "white matter."
> The result? A teen's brain gets faster and more efficient.

*"Changing what we watch on our inner TV screen is an option.
What you think, you make so.
Thoughts create.
Thoughts can be used to inspire or depress.
When we realize life is what we believe (and/or fear), we are able to change our minds."*

~ Betty Lou Lieber

Create what you want to believe, see, hear, and replay, about the main character – YOU!!

My Inner TV

TEENS – DISCOVERING IDENTITY AND MOVING TOWARD INDEPENDENCE

My Inner TV
FOR THE FACILITATOR

I. **Purpose**
   To compare thoughts to a television screen and depict and/or describe a positive personal *program*.

II. **Skills**
   Verbalize three or more ways the ability to control personal thoughts resembles a TV remote control.
   Personalize a quotation that uses a TV analogy. Explain the power of thoughts.
   Create what one wants to believe; see, hear and replay about self.
   Practice positive visualization concerning an upcoming challenge. Focus on behavior, not outcomes.
   Identify eight or more types of remote controls. List four or more ways they relate to types of thoughts.

III. **Possible Activities**
   a. Display a TV remote control or ask a volunteer to draw one on the board.
   b. Ask about its functions (channel, delete, enter, exit, format, guide, info, input, list, menu, mute, off, on, power, previous, record, volume, etc.).
   c. Pose the question: "How does a TV remote resemble ways we can control our own thoughts?"
      Possibilities
      • We can change TV channels and change our thoughts.
      • We can mute the TV and silence or replace negative self-talk.
      • We can select what to view from the menu or guide and decide what to focus on mentally.
   d. Distribute the *My Inner TV* handout.
   e. A volunteer reads the FACT aloud, encourages reactions, reads the quotation, and directions aloud.
   f. Encourage teens to use sketches, symbols, cartoons, words, etc., to show their beliefs and behavior.
   g. Allow time for completion.
   h. Encourage teens to share their responses and to receive peer feedback.
   i. Expect a variety of individual responses.

IV. **Enrichment Activities**
   a. Point out this portion of the quotation: "…*we are able to change our minds.*"
      • Explain that positive visualization can change our minds about ourselves.
      • Encourage teens to identify an upcoming challenge.
      • Prompt teens to describe images of themselves doing their best in the situations.
      • Emphasize that they envision their own behavior, not outcomes or others' reactions.
      • Caution teens to avoid focusing on factors over which they have no control.
   b. Ask teens to brainstorm types of remote controls other than TV devices. A peer lists their ideas.
      Possibilities

• Cameras	• Garage door openers	• Security systems
• Ceiling fan	• Lights	• Thermostats
• Games	• Music and other media	• Toys

   c. Suggest that teens divide into teams and develop lists that compare the devices with types of thoughts.
      Provide the following hints if necessary
      • Garage doors – List hopeful thoughts to be *open* to and hopeless thoughts to *shut* out.
      • Lights – List thoughts that *enlighten* (inspirational quotations) or *darken* (hatred, guilt).
      • Security systems – List thoughts that are *dangerous* (glamorizing illegal activities, substances).
      • Security Systems – List thoughts that are *protective* (support systems, self-esteem).
      • Thermostats – List thoughts that are *cold* (exclusion, discrimination, "It's all about me.").
      • Thermostats – List *warm* thoughts toward others ("They're doing the best they can") .

Cognitive Identity

BRAIN DEVELOPMENT

> **FACT**
> The teen brain totally rewires itself.
> The process is driven by thrill-seeking, risk-taking, and the need for approval from friends.
> These drives push teens to learn new skills that they will need to survive as adults.

Empower yourself to develop your brain, in a dynamic way.

Organization Team	**Skills Team**	**Brakes Team**
List three or more ways to organize thoughts. *Example: Decide what to do first.*	List three or more skills to develop that will help throughout life. *Examples: Basic math or anger management.*	List at least three ways to control impulses when angry, afraid or excited. *Example: Stop and think first.*
Planning Team	**Health Team**	**Steer Clear Team**
List three or more qualities to develop. *Example: Patience.*	List three or more ways to promote brain health. *Example: Sleep eight or more hours.*	List three or more actions to avoid. *Example: Drinking alcohol.*

TEENS – DISCOVERING IDENTITY AND MOVING TOWARD INDEPENDENCE

Brain Development
FOR THE FACILITATOR

I. Purpose
To recognize ways to develop the brain and identify activities that help or harm the brain's functions.

II. Skills
Identify three or more ways to enhance the brain's ability to do the following:
- Organize thoughts
- Develop skills
- Control impulses
- Plan ahead

State three ways to promote brain health and three actions that can harm the brain.

III. Possible Activities
a. Before the session, read b. below and decide whether to use the Interactive Team or the Independent Thinking Team Format. The size of the team can range from one to any number of people, depending on the size of the group.

b. For either format, distribute the *Brain Development* handout.
Ask a volunteer to read the FACT and encourage reactions. Other volunteers read the team descriptions.

Interactive Team Format
- Divide the group into six teams; team members sit together to confer.
- Team secretaries record their teams' ideas in the designated box.
- The group re-convenes and secretaries share their teams' lists.

Independent Thinking Team Format
- Divide the group into six teams; teens remain in their seats and do not confer with team members.
- Teens complete their assigned teams' lists independently.
- Then the team members form panels and go to the front of the room (one team at a time).
- Team members read their individual lists and receive peer feedback.

Possibilities

Organization Team	Skills Team	Brakes Team
Deep breathe and slow down	Academic subjects	Awareness of intense emotions
Write, draw or doodle thoughts	Safe driving	In the heat of the moment, think
List "Things To Do"	Music, art, sports, etc.	Talk about feelings
Use a calendar	Getting along with people	Avoid temptation
Think "First things first"	Self-awareness and control	Reward self-control

Planning Team	Health Team	Steer Clear Team
Compassion	Feed your brain healthy food	Mind-altering drugs
Generosity	Read	Negative self-talk
Gratitude	Physical exercise for the brain	Too much television and games
Honesty	Crosswords, puzzles, Sudoku	Riding without a helmet
Reliability	Online problem-solving games	Diving into shallow water

IV. Enrichment Activities
a. Encourage a discussion of the effects of sleep deprivation on the teen brain (irritability, impulsivity, depression, impaired judgment, slow reactions, and impaired physical and mental health).

b. Suggest that teens research and report the effects of alcohol on the teen brain (impaired learning and memory, greater risk for addiction, poor coordination and balance, decreased emotional control and increased risk for alcohol poisoning, injuries and death).

Cognitive Identity

Great Debates – Topics

> **FACT**
> The first nationally televised general election debates occurred in 1960 with John F. Kennedy and Richard Nixon.

Debate is a method of interactive discussion, basically an argument with rules.

**Debate helps raise graduation rates, boost college readiness and the chance to succeed in life.
Debate builds the Five Cs of 21st Century Skills …
Critical thinking, Communication, Collaboration, Creativity and Civic awareness.**

Select a topic from the list below or create your own topic for debate.

Abolish school dress codes.
Allow animal testing for new medicines.
Allow students to wear tee shirts with controversial messages because of freedom of speech.
Athletes must maintain a certain grade point average to stay on a team.
Ban smoking everywhere.
Destroy nuclear weapons worldwide.
Kill terrorists without holding a trial.
Legalize human cloning (produce an exact copy of a person).
Legalize marriage for teens under age 18.
Once "bad" in math (or any subject) always "bad" in math (or any subject).
Post anything on the Internet because of freedom of speech.
Provide sex education in middle schools.
Start and end school later in the day so teens can sleep longer.
Teens are too dependent on technology.
The fast food industry is responsible for obesity.
The media promotes risky behavior.
Throw professional sports players off the team for illegal activities in their personal lives.
Today's educational system needs no changes.
Video violence affects teen brains.

Decide whether you are for (pro) or against (con) the statement.

My own topic for debate is …

_____

_____

_____

Great Debates – Talk and Listen

Topic _____

Am I Pro or Con? _____

My reasons:

_____
_____
_____
_____
_____
_____
_____

My notes as I listen to my opponent's side:

_____
_____
_____
_____
_____
_____
_____

My comments to refute my opponent's opinions:

_____
_____
_____
_____
_____
_____
_____

Cognitive Identity

Great Debates – Quotations

"Minds are like parachutes — they only function when open." ~ Thomas Dewar

A situation in which my open mind functioned well …

_____
_____
_____
_____
_____
_____
_____

"Those who stand for nothing fall for anything." ~ Alexander Hamilton

The most important principle I stand for …

_____
_____
_____
_____
_____
_____
_____

Can a person be open-minded and still stand strongly?

I believe …

_____
_____
_____
_____
_____
_____
_____

TEENS – DISCOVERING IDENTITY AND MOVING TOWARD INDEPENDENCE

Great Debates
FOR THE FACILITATOR

I. **Purpose**
   To develop a cognitive identity as a person who thinks, speaks, listens and substantiates one's own opinions.

II. **Skills**
   Select a topic of interest from among twenty options.
   State whether one is *Pro* or *Con* and the reasons.
   Document an opponent's views.
   Rebut the opposing opinions.
   Discuss benefits of the Five C's of 21st Century Skills.

III. **Possible Activities**
   a. Ask how many teens have been in debates (with parents/care providers, on a formal team, etc.).
   b. Encourage a discussion about makes a great debate (opinions, open minds, respect, background facts).
   c. Distribute two of the handouts: *Great Debates Topics*, page 53, and *Great Debates, Talk and Listen*, page 54.
   d. A volunteer reads the FACT aloud and encourages reactions.
   e. Another volunteer reads the information, directions, and list of topics aloud.
   f. Teens decide on topics or create their own and complete the top third of *Talk* and *Listen*.
      Ideally for each topic selected, one or more teens will take the *Pro* and *Con* side.
      If more than one teen takes the same side of a topic they can become a debate team.
      If only one person selects a topic, a volunteer may play the opponent or the person may argue both sides and the group will guess whether the person is actually *Pro* or *Con*.
      Debate Rules
      • No personal attacks.
      • No winners or losers.
      • Teens who prefer not to speak may be team members who provide ideas to the debaters.
      • First speaker – one to three minutes.
      • Opponent – one to three minutes.
      • Time out as both review their notes and prepare rebuttals - one to three minutes
      • Rebuttals – one to three minutes for each side.
      • The audience applauds as each team concludes.
   g. When the session is over, ask teens to raise their hands if any of the debate(s) changed their opinions.
   h. Distribute the third handout *Great Debates - Quotations*, page 55.
   i. Volunteers read the quotations, sentence starters, and questions aloud.
   j. Allow time for completion; encourage teens to share their responses.
      Possibilities
      • Expect a variety of individualized responses as teens personalize the quotations.
      • *Can people be open-minded and still stand strongly?* Yes.
      • *I believe* – they can consider all sides of issues, then form and stick to their own opinions.

IV. **Enrichment Activities**
   a. Encourage interpretations of the *Five C's of 21st Century Skills* enhanced through debating.
      Possibilities
      • Critical Thinking – open-minded, informed by evidence; analyze and apply concepts.
      • Communication – exchange information, thoughts, and feelings.
      • Collaboration – work with team toward a common goal.
      • Creativity – invent something new; imagine unique ideas or techniques.
      • Civic awareness/engagement – understand community issues; act to benefit members.

Cognitive Identity ▶

BRAVER, STRONGER, AND SMARTER

> **FACT**
> Alan Alexander Milne is the creator of Winnie the Pooh.
> The book was inspired in part by the stuffed toys of Milne's son,
> Christopher Robin. Milne also authored the adult detective story
> The Red House Mystery.

"Promise me you'll remember you are BRAVER than you believe, STRONGER than you seem, SMARTER than you think."
— Christopher Robin to Pooh ~ A. A. Milne

Fill in the thought bubbles.

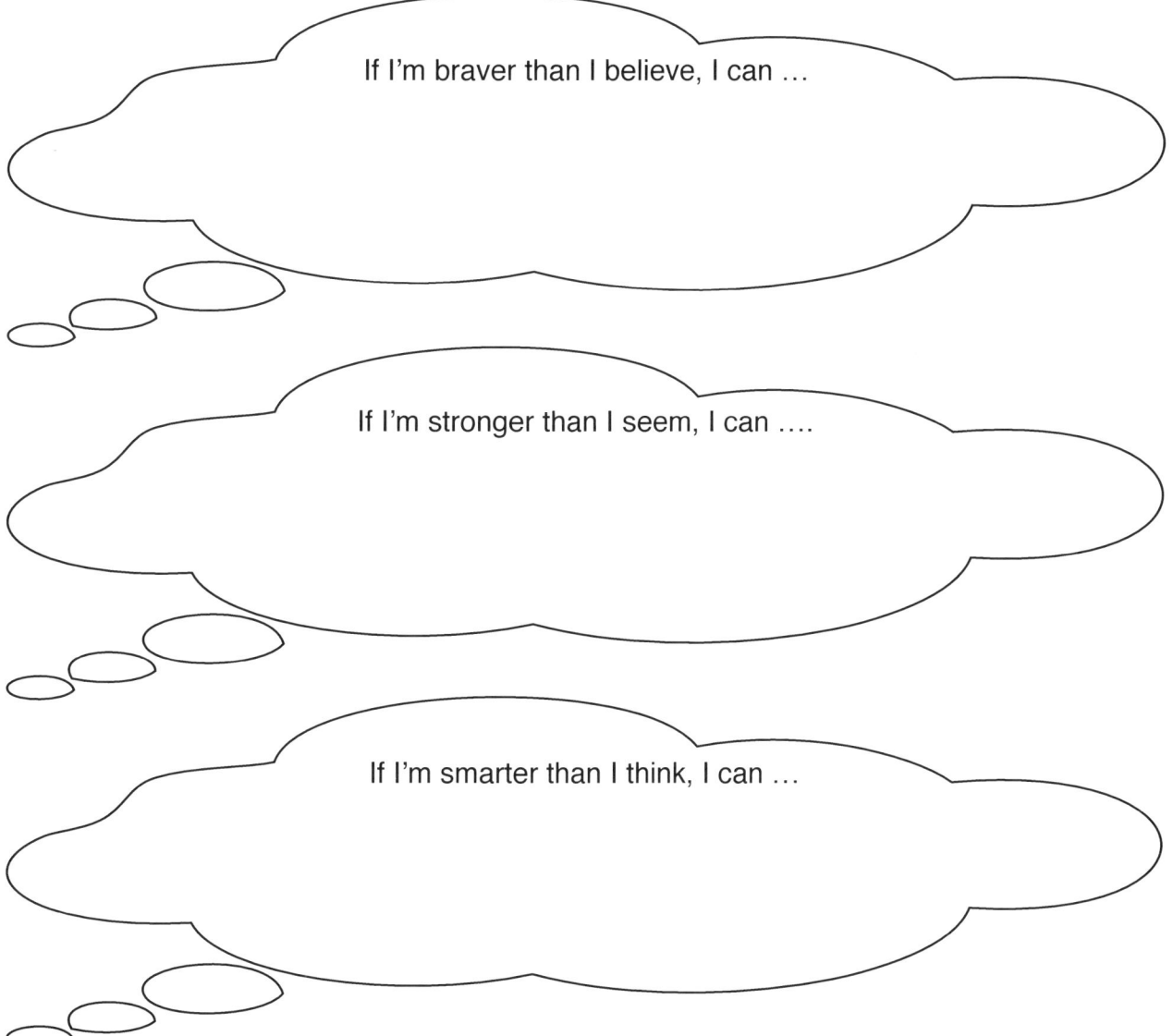

If I'm braver than I believe, I can …

If I'm stronger than I seem, I can ….

If I'm smarter than I think, I can …

TEENS – DISCOVERING IDENTITY AND MOVING TOWARD INDEPENDENCE

BRAVER, STRONGER, AND SMARTER
FOR THE FACILITATOR

I. Purpose
To use thoughts to promote positive actions.

II. Skills
Acknowledge the importance of thoughts and actions in establishing connections in the brain.
Identify five or more everyday ways to act brave, strong and smart.
State actions that can result from a person's belief in one's own bravery, strength and intellect.
Share personal actions being taken to cultivate different types of bravery, strength and intellect.
Imagine other ways to exemplify positive traits through actions.

III. Possible Activities
  a. Place three headings on the board or on paper taped to three walls of the room with these titles: "Everyday Ways to be Brave," "Everyday Ways to be Strong," and "Everyday Ways to be Smart."
  b. Explain that bravery is not necessarily saving a life; strength is not just muscle; and smart does not mean getting an "A."
  Elicit a few examples similar to the possibilities below before teens start.
  c. Prompt teens to walk around the room and add one idea to each list.
  d. Allow teens to circulate a few times, each teen adding one idea to each list per cycle.
  e. When teens are finished or after ten minutes, ask volunteers to read the lists aloud.

  Possibilities

  Everyday Ways to be Brave
  - Accept a challenge
  - Speak up for what's right
  - Act on unpopular convictions
  - Take on a task despite fear

  Everyday Ways to be Strong
  - Survive difficulties
  - Hear criticism with an open mind
  - Tell the truth
  - Use inner strength as well as a support system

  Everyday Ways to be Smart
  - Think of a new way to do something
  - Use common sense
  - Solve puzzles
  - Understand people
  - Learn from mistakes
  - Develop self-awareness
  - Ponder philosophies
  - Move with athletic ability
  - Appreciate and learn about nature

  f. Ask a volunteer to sketch a brain. Privately tell the teen to depict ridges and grooves.
  g. Explain that the grooves are pathways made by thoughts.
  h. Distribute the *Braver, Stronger and Smarter* handout.
  i. A volunteer reads the FACT aloud and encourages reactions.
  j. Another volunteer reads the quotation and directions aloud.
  k. Ask teens "What kinds of thoughts do you want to be repeated in your mind?" (Positive).
  l. Tell teens to be specific about the positive actions they will take when completing the thought bubbles.
  m. Allow time for completion.
  n. Encourage teens to share responses and to receive peer feedback.

IV. Enrichment Activities
Ask teens to share other examples of thoughts that foster positive actions (I have more self-esteem than I realize; I'm more creative than I think; I'm more compassionate than I seem.).

Cognitive Identity

I Have Learned ...

FACT
Most people remember 10-20 per cent of what they **HEAR**,
however, they do remember 80-90 per cent of what they
SAY and DO.

**We are all in the process of becoming experts in something.
The more knowledge we share with others, the more we learn.**

People were asked what they have learned about life.
"I've learned our dog doesn't want to eat my broccoli either." Age 7
"I've learned that to cheer yourself up, try cheering someone else up." Age 14
"I've learned that silent company is often more healing than words of advice." Age 24

Write about something that you have learned about life.

I have learned _____
_____
_____

I have learned _____
_____
_____

I have learned _____
_____
_____

✂ -

Write about some things you hope to learn about life.

_____
_____
_____
_____
_____
_____

TEENS – DISCOVERING IDENTITY AND MOVING TOWARD INDEPENDENCE

I Have Learned …
FOR THE FACILITATOR

I. **Purpose**
   To introspect about life's lessons learned to date, share wisdom with peers, and look toward the future.

II. **Skills**
   Identify three concepts learned in life.
   Describe one or more thing hoped to learn in the future.
   Share knowledge and questions about life with peers.

III. **Possible Activities**
   a. Ask teens how they usually respond when asked "What did you learn at school today?"
   b. Pose the question "What have you learned outside of school today?"
      (Expect varied responses).
   c. Distribute the *I Have Learned …* handout.
   d. A volunteer reads the FACT aloud and encourages reactions.
   e. Other volunteers read information, examples, and directions aloud.
   f. Ask for an example response for *some things you hope to learn about life.*
      - Expect superficial responses. *Ex*: Why does it rain on prom night?
      - Expect serious responses. *Ex*: Why do bad things happen to good people?
   g. Explain that some of life's unknowns may seem to have no answers, which may or may not be revealed in the future.
   h. Allow time for completion.
   i. Encourage volunteers to share their responses to one or more of the *I have learned …* prompts.
   j. Volunteers may receive and/or give feedback.

IV. **Enrichment Activity**
   Promote an "It Remains Unknown" activity.
   Choose one of the formats:

   "It Remains Unknown" Paper Pass Format
   - Volunteers cut or tear the bottom portion (broken line) of the handout where they identified what they hope to learn about life.
   - The pieces of paper are distributed to peers.
   - Each person who has a possible answer to the unknown writes a response on the back of the paper.
   - If a person has no answer, the person can write, "I wonder about that too."
   - After a specified time the facilitator says "Stop."
   - Whoever holds a paper, reads the "It Remains Unknown" and responds aloud.

   "It Remains Unknown" Brainstorming Format
   - Volunteers cut or tear the bottom portion of the handout where they identified their "unknown."
   - The pieces of paper are collected and placed at the front of the room.
   - Tell teens that when it is their turn they will do the following:
      Pick up an "unknown."
      Read it aloud.
      Encourage peers to share possible answers.

   For Both Formats
   - Remind teens that some "unknowns" are centuries old and may not be solved by the group.
   - Elicit that for some "unknowns," it helps to know that peers also wonder about the same issues.
   - Discuss that there are new "unknowns" with each step forward we make.

SOCIAL IDENTITY 5

Life is partly what we make it, and partly what it is made by the friends we choose.
~ Tehyi Hsieh

Take Chances with Friends? .... page 63 ▶

Teens acknowledge that they may take chances with friends around, and take chances by befriending people who exert negative pressure. Teens resist negative peer pressure and promote positive influences.

What's In My Cell Phone? .... page 65 ▶

Teens compare current priorities to future priorities and shift them as desired for the future. Teens identify four or more places and/or personal spaces whose contents do or do not reflect their future priorities.

SOCIAL CIRCLES .... page 67 ▶

Teens recognize aspects of self-identity, group identity, and the influences of groups on identity. Teens discuss or write about ways that by belonging to certain groups, they may benefit or jeopardize their well-being.

I Feel Most Lonely When… .... page 69 ▶

Teens identify situations that may contribute to loneliness and ways to overcome loneliness. Teens compose a "When You Feel Most Lonely … Letter" to help and inspire a fictitious person, self, and/or others.

Chapter 5 – Social Identity Skills

Throughout the chapter, teens will communicate through oral, written, and graphic expression, and give and receive feedback.

Teens: Skills in each activity.
Facilitators: Competencies to evaluate.

Take Chances with Friends?
- Acknowledge that teens tend to take more risks in the presence of peers.
- Participate in a supervised experiment to see if a volunteer gives in to subtle peer pressure.
- Demonstrate ways to avoid and/or handle negative peer pressure and promote positive influences through one or more of the following modes:
    Mock videos and/or role plays
    Brainstorm
    Game creation and participation
    Essays, song lyrics and/or poems
    Sketches or cartoons

What's In My Cell Phone?
- Depict and/or describe the contents of one's cell phone.
- Rank order them into three categories.
- State ways the cell phone's content priorities reflect what is wanted in the future.
- Identify ways the cell phone's contents are not indicative of what teens want their lives to represent.
- Discuss four or more other places whose contents do or do not reflect priorities.

Social Circles
- Identify five membership groups which are important to personal identity.
- Demonstrate the percent of self-identity encompassed by each of the five group memberships.
- Describe the positive and/or negative effects of each group on self-identity.
- Identify two or more reasons people join groups that negatively influence members and/or outsiders.
- Discuss one or more ways group membership can jeopardize and/or enhance personal well-being.

I Feel Most Lonely When …
- Select situations that trigger lonely feelings from a list of forty one or more.
- Identify additional lonely situations if applicable.
- Collaborate with peers to find one or more positive ways to cope with each lonely situation.
- Provide advice and inspiration by writing a letter to a fictitious person, then reading it to yourself.
- Share ideas with others by giving letters anonymously to peers or to others who may benefit.
- Connect with peers by jointly compiling articles and resources to help people overcome loneliness.
- Consider volunteering for a humanitarian organization to increase feelings of community and purpose.

Social Identity

Take Chances with Friends?

> **FACT**
> In a recent study, scientific tests showed that teens who
> play a driving simulation video game alone, and then play with friends watching,
> take double the risks in the presence of peers.

Sometimes just knowing peers are watching, influences teens in positive or negative ways.

Enjoy the presence of peers as you join one of these teams.

The Persuaders
Two or more players: Make a pretend video to teach younger children about peer pressure.

The Independents
Individuals: Write essays or draw sketches or cartoons to show aspects of negative and positive pressure. Then as a team they present their work.

The Perilous Peers
Pairs of players: Portray someone exerting negative peer pressure and a person resisting.

The Positive Peers
Pairs of players: Portray someone exerting positive peer pressure and a person complying.

The Brain-stormers
Any number of players: List ways to counteract negative peer pressure.

The Friends
Any number of players: List ways to find friends who will provide positive influences.

The Slip Ups
Any number of players: Write examples of negative peer pressure on slips of paper. Put the slips of paper into a container. Later people from other teams will read them aloud and state how they would handle the situations.

The Lyricists
Two or more players: Collaborate on poems or lyrics about positive influences and negative peer pressure.

TEENS – DISCOVERING IDENTITY AND MOVING TOWARD INDEPENDENCE

Take Chances with Friends?
FOR THE FACILITATOR

I. Purpose
To acknowledge that teens *take chances* with friends around and they *take chances* by befriending people who exert negative peer pressure.
To resist negative peer pressure and promote positive peer influences.

II. Skills
Acknowledge that teens tend to take more risks in the presence of peers.
Participate in a supervised experiment to see if a volunteer gives in to subtle peer pressure.
Demonstrate ways to avoid and/or handle negative peer pressure and promote positive influences through one or more of the following modes:

Brainstorm	Essays, song lyrics and/or poems
Game creation and participation	Mock videos
Role plays	Sketches or cartoons

III. Possible Activities
a. Plan that each activity may take more than one session.
b. Ask for a volunteer to leave the room for a few minutes.
c. Coach all peers to hold a hand over one eye.
d. Tell teens if the volunteer asks what is going on to shrug shoulders and continue covering one eye.
e. The volunteer enters the room.
f. The experiment continues a few minutes to see if the volunteer also covers an eye.
g. The volunteer shares how it felt to see everyone doing the same thing and the temptation to copy.
h. Encourage a brief discussion of activities teens are more likely to engage in when peers are present.
   Possibilities
   - Unsafe driving
   - Drinking alcohol, taking drugs and smoking
   - Violence and bullying
i. Distribute the *Take Chances with Friends?* handout.
j. A volunteer reads the FACT aloud, encourages reactions, and then reads the page aloud.
k. Assign teens to teams or allow them to choose.
l. Teens separate into teams and prepare their responses.
m. After a designated time, the group re-convenes.
n. All teams, except The Slip Ups, present their responses.
o. A member of The Slip Ups takes the container with slips of paper/situations to the front of the room.
p. Peers take turns reading the situations aloud and responding.

IV. Enrichment Activities
Review any of the following techniques to counter peer pressure that were not addressed by teens.
- Consider the consequences, not just the short term rewards, of trying to look *cool*.
- Don't cross the thin line between living life to the fullest and losing life.
- Find friends who enjoy new and exciting but safer activities (sports, amusement park thrills).
- Avoid people and situations in which unsafe actions are promoted.
- Seek role models who enjoy life and take positive risks (start a band, take an acting class).
- Say "No" and be proud to do what is right for you.
- Practice assertiveness methods. ("When you pressure me, I feel irritated, so please stop.")
- Become a crusader for positive peer pressure and experience a *leadership high*.
- Join with peers for a *natural high* (volunteer for charities, suggest new programs to administrators).

Social Identity

What's In My Cell Phone?

> **FACT**
> On September 21, 1983, history was made when the FCC approved the 8000X, the world's first commercial portable cell phone. It cost consumers $3,995 at the time. (Which would be almost $10,000 in 2015.) It weighed about 2 pounds and the battery took ten hours to charge.

**Draw an outline of your cell phone below.
Sketch, symbolize and/or use words for the following:**
In most of the space, show what your phone is used for most of the time.
In some of the space, show what your phone is used for some of the time.
In the smallest space, squeeze in what your phone is used for least often.

How does your cell phone reflect what you want your life to represent in the future?

_____
_____
_____

How is your cell phone NOT indicative of what you want your life to represent in the future?

_____
_____
_____

What's In My Cell Phone?
FOR THE FACILITATOR

I. **Purpose**
   To compare current priorities to future priorities.
   To shift priorities as desired for the future.

II. **Skills**
   Depict and/or describe the items in one's cell phone.
   Rank order them into three categories.
   State ways the phone priorities reflect what is wanted in their future life.
   Identify ways the phone's contents are not indicative of what teens want their lives to represent.
   Discuss four or more other places whose contents do or do not reflect priorities.

III. **Possible Activities**
   a. Ask teens to access their cell phones.
   b. Encourage teens to share what they like about having a cell phone.
   c. Distribute the *What's In My Cell Phone?* handout.
   d. A volunteer reads the FACT aloud, encourages reactions, and reads the directions aloud.
   e. Allow time for completion.
   f. Encourage teens to share responses and to receive peer feedback.
   Possibilities
   Expect a variety of individual responses.
   How does your cell phone reflect what you want your life to represent in the future?
   - Many communications are to family, and close family ties are wanted.
   - Information about universities has been researched, and a college education is wanted.

   How is your cell phone not indicative of what you want your life to represent in the future?
   - Many phone calls are to drug dealers and a healthy lifestyle is wanted.
   - Many texts are degrading to partner and a loving relationship is wanted.

IV. **Enrichment Activity**
   a. Pose the question: "What do some people make a big deal about that may be *small stuff?*" (Connecting with people 24/7. Basing popularity on who has the latest cell phone. A relationship with someone who doesn't care).
   b. Ask: "What do some people minimize that may be important?" (Inclusion and diversity. Keeping in touch with family. Education and career. Random acts of kindness).
   c. Write "Nomophobia" on the board and ask its meaning (fear of being without cell phone contact).
   Many people without cell phone contact experience extreme amounts of stress.
   d. Encourage teens to share stories of times they lost their phones, ran out of battery charge or credit.
   e. Suggest that teens identify other places whose contents do or do not reflect their future priorities.
   Possibilities
   - Backpack
   - Bedroom
   - Journal
   - Vehicle

Social Identity

SOCIAL CIRCLES

> **FACT**
> Being in a group helped early humans survive. They protected each other, hunted and cooked together, and endured harsh environments. Today, even with walls and clothes, most people feel safer with others around.

Create smiley faces on the five blank circles below to represent you.

Label each of the five other circles with the most important groups to which you belong or want to join.

Then cut out the circles.

TEENS – DISCOVERING IDENTITY AND MOVING TOWARD INDEPENDENCE

SOCIAL CIRCLES

FOR THE FACILITATOR

I. **Purpose**
To recognize aspects of self-identity, group identity, and the influences of groups on identity.

II. **Skills**
Identify five groups in which membership is important to personal identity.
Demonstrate the percent of self-identity encompassed by each of the five group memberships.
Describe the positive and/or negative effects of each group on self-identity.
Identify two or more reasons people join groups that negatively influence members and/or outsiders.
Identify one or more ways group membership can jeopardize and/or enhance personal well-being.

III. **Possible Activities**
   a. Before the session, obtain scissors.
   b. At the start of the session, ask teens to brainstorm groups to which they belong. A volunteer lists ideas.
   Possibilities
   - Clique
   - Club
   - Dating partnership
   - Ethnic, racial, religious, spiritual
   - Family
   - Friends
   - Gender, gender identity, sexual orientation
   - Mutual interest group – band, chorus, martial arts class
   - Online communities
   - Political or activist
   - Sports team
   - Volunteer or community service
   - Work

   c. Distribute the *Social Circles* handout. A volunteer reads the FACT aloud, encourages reactions, and then reads directions aloud.
   d. Allow time for completion.
   e. Ask teens to estimate the amount of their self-identity that is tied into the membership in each group.
   f. Direct teens to place the group circles over their smiley faces accordingly.
   g. Provide examples:
      - An athlete who is totally absorbed in the sport might have eighty percent of self-identity tied up in being a member of the team. Eighty percent of the smiley face is covered by the "Team" circle.
      - A person in a foster home who sees biological relatives once a week may have twenty-five percent of self-identity tied up in family of origin. One fourth of the face is covered by the "Family" circle.
   h. Encourage teens to take turns going to the front of the room and showing how much of their self-identities are tied up in each social group they consider important.
   i. Ask teens to take turns describing each group's positive and/or negative effects on them.
      Possibilities
      (–) Friends may influence them to totally accept in-group members but put down outsiders.
      (+) Fellow band members may influence them to practice daily and play their best.

IV. **Enrichment Activities**
Encourage discussions or essays about the following topics:
   - Why do people join groups that harm members or outsiders emotionally or physically?
     (A charismatic leader, the promise of acceptance).
   - How can allegiance to a group jeopardize well-being?
     (Substance abuse or fighting are required for acceptance).
   - How can membership in a group benefit one's well-being?
     (Time and talents are focused on productive activities in a school club or service organization).

Social Identity

I Feel Most Lonely When … Checklist

> **FACT**
> Loneliness is not the same as being alone,
> in fact a person can feel lonely when surrounded by others, even loved ones.
> Aloneness is different. Some people love it – some do not.

I feel most lonely when …

Family
- ☐ A family member is ill and I must devote my time.
- ☐ A member of my family is disappointed in me.
- ☐ My family isn't there for me.
- ☐ I am home.
- ☐ I think about a certain person at home.
- ☐ A family member is no longer with us.

Friends
- ☐ My friend talks about self-harm and I don't know how to help.
- ☐ My friends are doing something I don't want to do and they try to make me feel bad.
- ☐ My friends aren't there for me.
- ☐ My friends do things without including me.
- ☐ My friends don't agree with me.
- ☐ My friends on social media seem to be having so much fun.
- ☐ I can't talk on my cell phone or go onto social media.
- ☐ Good friends don't like my behavior.
- ☐ I lost a friend.

Relationships
- ☐ After I get together with some random person.
- ☐ I have no one special to love.
- ☐ I lost a partner
- ☐ Someone I like doesn't like me.
- ☐ My sexuality is questioned.

School
- ☐ I am at school.
- ☐ I am dropped from a team or group.
- ☐ I feel stupid in class.
- ☐ I move and have to change schools.
- ☐ I eat lunch alone.
- ☐ I am bullied and bystanders do nothing to help.
- ☐ I see someone being bullied and I don't know what to do.

Thoughts
- ☐ I am judged.
- ☐ I am considered different from others.
- ☐ I am ill.
- ☐ I am ignored.
- ☐ I am alone in a crowd.
- ☐ People make fun of me.
- ☐ I am left out of a group of people.
- ☐ I am surrounded by people whose values are different from mine.
- ☐ I have no one to talk with about a problem.
- ☐ I defend what I believe and no one agrees.
- ☐ I say I need help and am ignored.
- ☐ People belittle me.
- ☐ People don't care about what I have to say.
- ☐ People don't understand me.
- ☐ _____

(Add additional situations on the back of the page).

I Feel Most Lonely When ... Ways to Cope

Brainstorm with teammates and list everyone's ideas of ways to cope.

Family Team – Ways to cope

___

Friends – Ways to Cope

___

Relationships – Ways to Cope

___

School – Ways to Cope

___

Thoughts – Ways to Cope

___

Social Identity

When You Feel Most Lonely ... Letter

Write an anonymous letter to a fictitious person who feels lonely and ...
Suggest ways to cope.
Instill hope with inspirational words and/or quotations.
Then, read the letter to yourself.
You may choose to share it with people who may benefit from your letter.

Dear _____,

TEENS – DISCOVERING IDENTITY AND MOVING TOWARD INDEPENDENCE

I Feel Most Lonely When …
FOR THE FACILITATOR

I. Purpose
To identify situations that may contribute to loneliness and ways to overcome loneliness.

II. Skills
Select situations that trigger personal lonely feelings from a list of forty-one or more. Identify additional situations if applicable. Collaborate with peers to find one or more positive ways to cope with each situation. Provide advice and inspiration by writing a letter to a fictitious person, then reading it to self. Share ideas with others by giving letters anonymously to peers or to others who may benefit. Connect with peers by jointly compiling articles and resources to help people overcome loneliness. Consider volunteering for a humanitarian organization to increase feelings of community and purpose.

III. Possible Activities
  a. Plan to present the three *I Feel Most Lonely When …* handouts during the same or consecutive sessions.
  b. Ask teens to share feelings about songs that address loneliness.
  c. Plan to distribute the handouts one at a time. Complete each handout before the next is presented.
  - ***I Feel Most Lonely When … Checklist***, page 69.
    A volunteer reads the FACT aloud and encourages reactions.
    Teens check boxes that relate to them and add items at the bottom and/or on the back of the page. Allow time for completion.
  - ***I Feel Most Lonely When … Ways to Cope***, page 70.
    Explain that teens will brainstorm ways to cope with each situation.
    Teens select the most relevant team: Family, Friends, Relationships, School, Thoughts.
    Teammates sit together to brainstorm coping techniques.
    Teammates list each other's ideas on their handouts under the pertinent heading.
    The group re-convenes.
    Teens share their teams' insights.
    Each team's most legible list may be photocopied for peers. Then, all have a skills list for all topics.
  - ***When You Feel Most Lonely … Letter***, page 71.
    A volunteer reads the directions aloud.
    Allow time for completion.
    Encourage teens to read their letters aloud and to receive peer feedback.
    Suggest that teens fold their letters and place them in a container.
    The container is passed around and each teen picks up a folded letter and keeps it.
    Alternatively, volunteers may allow their letters to be photocopied and distributed to all.
  d. Summarize the session by emphasizing these truths:
    Teens may not be able to change a situation but they can revise their thinking about it.
    Loneliness combined with anger, sadness, or isolation, requires professional help.

IV. Enrichment Activities
  a. Motivate teens to collect articles from reliable resources about coping with loneliness.
    - Prompt teens to work together to compile a notebook of articles and resources.
    - Suggest they give the notebook to a teacher or counselor to photocopy for the group and to make available for other teens.
  b. Encourage teens to connect with people and feel needed by volunteering at a local humanitarian organization or for a particular cause that interests them.

SPIRITUAL IDENTITY 6

To have faith is to trust yourself to the water. When you swim, you don't grab hold of the water, because if you do you will sink and drown. Instead, you relax and float.

~ Alan Watts

Scared? .... page 75 ▶
Teens redirect fear to invent, create, and propel positive activities. Teens recognize that some fears are worth continuing because they promote safe actions..

Fly Like A Kite .... page 77 ▶
Teens apply simple aerodynamic principles in order to reach their personal maximum potentials. Teens compare the kite's connection to the person who controls it, and then to their connections to positive people, places, and things.

My Storm .... page 81 ▶
Teens learn ways to adopt a calm mindset amidst a chaotic situation. Teens compare current thoughts, feelings, and actions with positive thoughts, feelings, and actions. They learn to use imagery to create the calm in the center of personal storms.

Chapter 6 – Spiritual Identity Skills

Throughout the chapter, teens will communicate through oral, written, and graphic expression, and give and receive feedback.

Teens: Skills in each activity.
Facilitators: Competencies to evaluate.

Scared?
- Identify a personal, major fear.
- Describe an invention or opportunity to use the fear to improve personal and/or community life.
- Create a product, campaign, or artistic representation that helps others who experience the fear.
- State a way to be propelled to productive action.
- Try new strategies despite a fear.
- Suggest three or more interventions to help peers use personal fears for positive purposes.
- Identify four or more words related to fear and faith.
- Supply a new concept for each letter in each word by creating an acrostic.

Fly like A Kite
- Represent personal positive qualities and future goals and hopes in the form of a soaring kite.
- Compare twelve kite-flying facts to personal factors that promote and/or deter self-actualization.
- Give two or more examples from among three categories of connections that help the teen succeed.
- Represent a personal legacy by drawing a streamer or banner labeled with qualities, lessons, messages, etc.

My Storm
- Describe a difficult or stormy personal situation and the related thoughts, feelings and actions.
- Document one or more positive thoughts, feelings and actions related to the same situation.
- Re-create a calm eye of the storm using imagery and words.
- Identify four or more different types of emotional storms and one or more ways to cope with each.
- Compose one or more sentences that a personified calm in the center of the storm would say.

Spiritual Identity ▶

Scared?

> **FACT**
> Horror movies, video villains, haunted houses and roller coasters appeal to many people. A "scare specialist" sociologist found that the brain chemicals released during scary activities give some people a fabulous "kick." Surviving scary situations also boosts self-esteem when survivors say: "Yes. I did it!"

What do Thomas Edison and Gustav Eiffel have in common?

FEAR

Thomas Edison, afraid of darkness, invented the light bulb.
Gustave Eiffel, afraid of heights, helped design and build the Eiffel Tower.
Many entertainers, afraid of public speaking, perform for crowds.
Amusement ride, game, and movie producers make millions by creating thrills and chills.

You, too, can capitalize on your fears. You can:
Invent
Create
Be propelled

Examples:

You are afraid of not fitting in with fashion.
- **Invent** your own trademark style.
- **Create** a campaign for students to donate fashionable clothes to shelters.
- **Be propelled** to wear clothes that defy the current fashion.

You are afraid of being told "No."
- **Invent** opportunities to experience "No." Soon you'll find it less scary. Soon there may be a "Yes."
- **Create** a story, poem, screenplay, comedy, game, etc. about a person who fears the word "No."
- **Be propelled** to try new ways to state wants and needs, ask different people, and make different requests.

One of my main fears is_____

I can invent _____

_____

I can create _____

_____

I can be propelled to _____

> **Some fears are legitimate and life-saving!**
> **They should NOT be re-invented, or re-created, but should propel SAFE actions.**

TEENS – DISCOVERING IDENTITY AND MOVING TOWARD INDEPENDENCE

Scared?
FOR THE FACILITATOR

I. Purpose
To re-direct fear to invent, create and propel productive activities.
To recognize that some fears are worth continuing because they promote safe actions.

II. Skills
Identify a personal, major fear.
Describe an invention or opportunity to use the fear to improve personal and/or community life.
Create a product, campaign, or artistic representation that helps others who experience the fear.
State a way to be propelled to productive action.
Try new strategies despite a fear.
Suggest three or more interventions to help peers use their fears for positive purposes.
Identify four or more words related to fear and faith.
Supply a new concept for each letter in each word by creating an acrostic.

III. Possible Activities
a. Before the session, secretly enlist a teen to drop a book or make a loud noise shortly after the session starts.
b. At the start of the session ask teens about their favorite types of entertainment.
c. As they talk, the peer makes the noise to startle people.
d. The teen who scared them admits it was part of an experiment – to see their reactions.
e. Resume the discussion about favorite types of entertainment.
Elicit scary types of entertainment teens seek out (Halloween haunted houses, sci-fi-films, etc.).
f. Distribute the *Scared?* handout. A volunteers reads the FACT aloud and encourages reactions. Another volunteer reads the information and examples aloud.
g. Allow time for completion.
h. Encourage teens to share their responses and to receive peer feedback.
i. Expect a variety of individual responses.

IV. Enrichment Activities
Suggest a *Fearless Fest* to have fun with the words related to overcoming fear.
As a board activity, as individuals, or in teams, teens develop acrostics.
Possibilities

FEAR
F – False
E – Expectations
A – Appear
R – Real

TRUST
T – To
R – Really
U – Understand
S – Scariness
T – Today

FAITH
F – Find
A – Acceptance
I – In
T – Trust and
H – Hope

BRAVE
B – Boldly
R – Recognize
A – Achievements
V – Victoriously
E – Everyday

Spiritual Identity ▶

Fly Like a Kite: Me

FACT
Each year, on the second Sunday of October, kite flyers in nearly every country of the world unite to fly a kite, to celebrate "One sky, one world."

**Imagine that you are a kite in all its glory:
Magnificently colored
Able to fly**

Write your responses on the kite below. Then decorate it with your favorite colors.

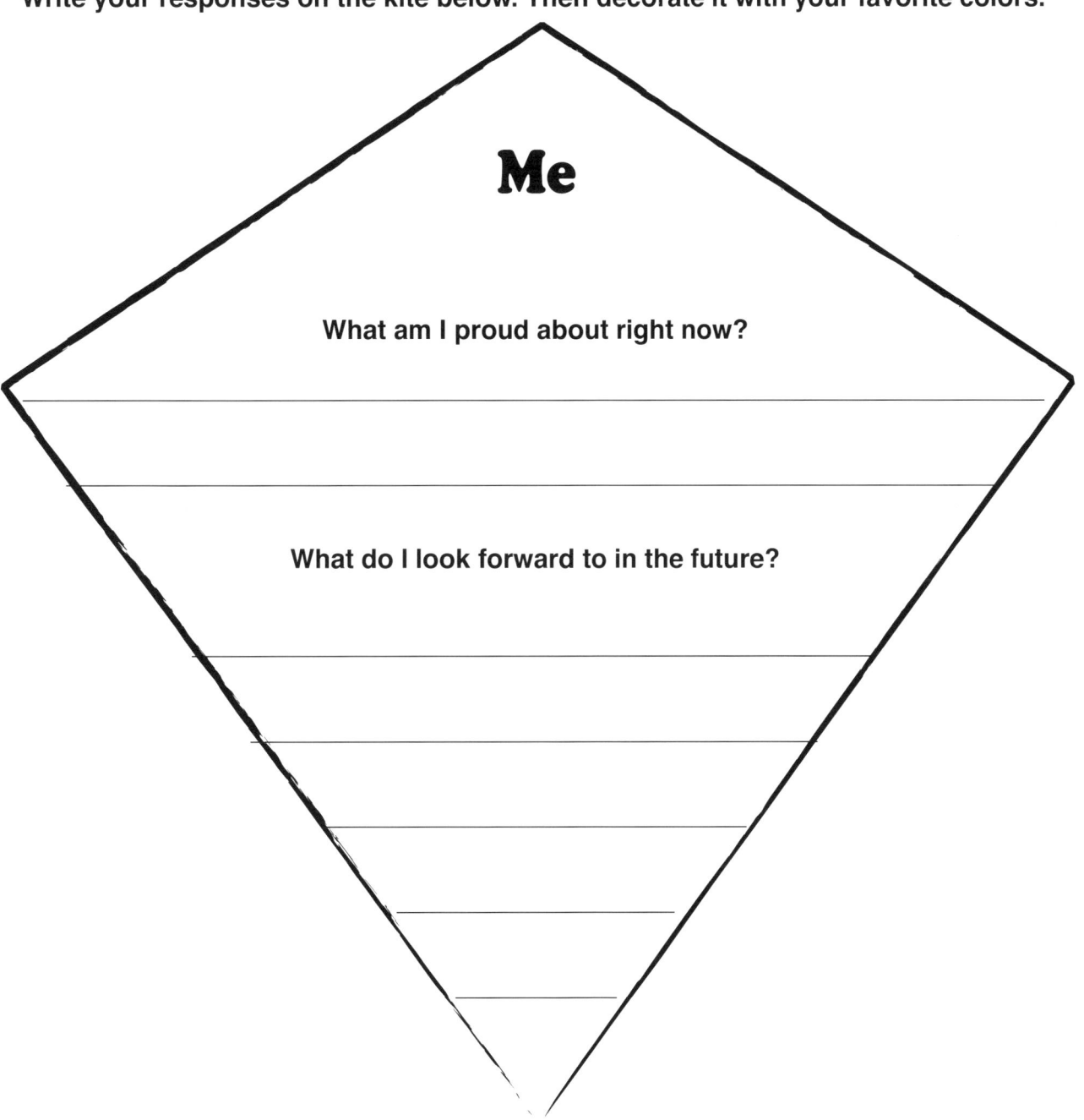

Me

What am I proud about right now?

What do I look forward to in the future?

© 2015 WHOLE PERSON ASSOCIATES, 101 W. 2ND ST., SUITE 203, DULUTH MN 55802 • 800-247-6789

Fly Like a Kite: Comparisons

Find ways you are like a kite by noting your ideas in the "About Me" column.

About Kites	About Me
People want their kites to fly high.	Who and what help me reach my highest goals?
Lift is the upward force of air under a kite.	Who and what lift my hopes?
Thrust is the forward push.	Who and what push me forward?
Weight is the downward force of gravity.	Who and what hold me down?
Drag is the backward force.	Who and what drag me backward?
Kites fly against the wind.	Who and what are the winds I am up against?
Kites use the wind to their advantage.	How can I use the opposing wind to my advantage?
Kites need a balance of forces to stay in the air.	How can I be in better balance?
Kite flyers control their own kites.	What can I control about my present and future?
Kite flyers exert tension on the string.	What types of tension will help me?
Kites can crash and tear.	What can I do if my goals and hopes crash?
With no wind, flyers run to jump-start their kites.	How can I jump start my goals and hopes?

Spiritual Identity ▶

Fly Like a Kite: Connections and Memories

A kite is connected to one person who controls it.

Most people need more than one connection to fly their highest.

Describe types of people, places, personal qualities, and values that help you soar.

People _____

_____

_____

Places _____

_____

_____

Personal Qualities and Values _____

_____

_____

Imagine the kite's tail as its legacy and as what is last seen and remembered about the kite.

What legacy or gifts will you leave to your world?

Examples:
How do you inspire people?
What lessons have you learned that will help others?
What are your motivational messages?
What mark on the world will you create?

**Draw your kite's long swirling streamer or banner below.
In your streamer, write what you want people to remember about you.**

TEENS – DISCOVERING IDENTITY AND MOVING TOWARD INDEPENDENCE

Fly Like a Kite
FOR THE FACILITATOR

I. **Purpose**
   To apply simple aerodynamic principles to reaching a personal maximum potential.

II. **Skills**
   Represent personal positive qualities and future goals and hopes in the form of a soaring kite. Compare twelve kite-flying facts to personal factors that promote and/or deter self-actualization. Give two or more examples from among three categories of connections that help one succeed. Represent a personal legacy by drawing a streamer/banner labeled with qualities, lessons, messages, and/or illustrations of the teen's prospective *mark* on the world.

III. **Possible Activities**
   a. Plan to present the three handouts during the same or consecutive sessions. Provide color highlighters.
   b. Ask a volunteer to demonstrate how to make and fly a paper plane in less than five minutes.
   c. Explain that teens will be thinking about factors that cause objects to fly.
   d. Distribute the *Fly Like a Kite* handouts one at a time. Complete each before the next is presented.
   Me, page 77.
   - A volunteer reads the FACT aloud, encourages reactions, and reads the directions.
   - Encourage a discussion of teens' experiences with kites for recreation and sports (hang-gliders, etc.).
   - Allow time for completion.
   - Encourage teens to show and tell about their kites.
   - Expect a variety of personal responses.
   Possibilities
   What am I proud about right now? My honesty, compassion, efforts to develop specific abilities.
   What do I look forward to in the future? The person I am becoming, reaching my goals.
   Comparisons, page 78.
   - A volunteer reads the directions aloud.
   - Allow time for completion.
   - Encourage teens to share their responses.
   Possibilities (key words for the prompts are listed below in order)
   Reach my highest goal, lift my hopes, push me forward – teacher, positive self-talk, education, volunteerism.
   Hold me down, drag me backward – friends who take drugs, put-downs, negative thinking, time wasters.
   Winds I am up against – destructive criticism. Lack of funds, time, energy, supportive people.
   Use the opposing wind to my advantage – ignore negativity, hear constructive criticism, learn from mistakes.
   Better balance – work and play, interact and introspect. Religious and/or spiritual activities.
   Control of my present and future – my thoughts, feelings and actions.
   Tension that will help me – enough tension to energize me to study, work, plan, persist.
   If my goals and hopes crash – repair the damage, create new goals, change self, seek support.
   Jump-start my goals and hopes – Use inner strength. Ask advice from people who have *been there - done that.*
   Connections, page 79.
   People – people who believe I can achieve, expect the best, trust, nurture, guide, empathize.
   Places – caring environments in schools, houses of worship, homes, workplaces.
   Things – honesty with self and others, hard work, medical/mental health, training, experience.
   The kite's tail, streamer or banner – expect a variety of individual responses (from being a caring person or good parent to curing a disease or promoting world peace).

IV. **Enrichment Activities**
   a. Encourage teens to research simple ways to make their own kites.
   b. Allow time at a subsequent session to create kites and label them with uplifting words, phrases, symbols.
   c. Create a bulletin board of the kites teens completed on the *Me* page, or the kites they have made.

Spiritual Identity ▶

My Storm: My Situation Part I

> **FACT**
> In the center of a fierce hurricane is a small area where the weather is calm, the sky is clear, the winds are just light breezes. This area is called "the eye of the storm."

Your storm is your difficulty.
Share what's swirling around you.
Describe how you may feel churned up inside.

The stormy situation I am dealing with right now is …

_____

_____

_____

_____

My thoughts about it are …

_____

_____

_____

_____

My feelings about it are …

_____

_____

_____

_____

My recent actions have been to …

_____

_____

_____

_____

(Continued on the next page)

My Storm: My Situation Part II

Your situation has not changed. You can change your thoughts, feelings and actions related to the situation. You can be calm inside, no matter what happens outside.

(Continuation of my same situation on the previous page)

My more positive thoughts about my situation are …

_____
_____
_____
_____
_____
_____

My more positive feelings are …

_____
_____
_____
_____
_____
_____

My more positive actions will be to …

_____
_____
_____
_____
_____
_____

My Storm: My Calm Place

Life, in general, has storms – times when troubles seem to surround each of us.
You can be *the eye of the storm*, the calm in the middle of chaos.
Imagine the outer circle is your stormy situation.
The inner circle represents your calm mind.

Fill the inner circle with positive concepts that comfort you.
Examples:
Images (the beach)
Ideas (faith)
People (best friend)
Actions (meditation)

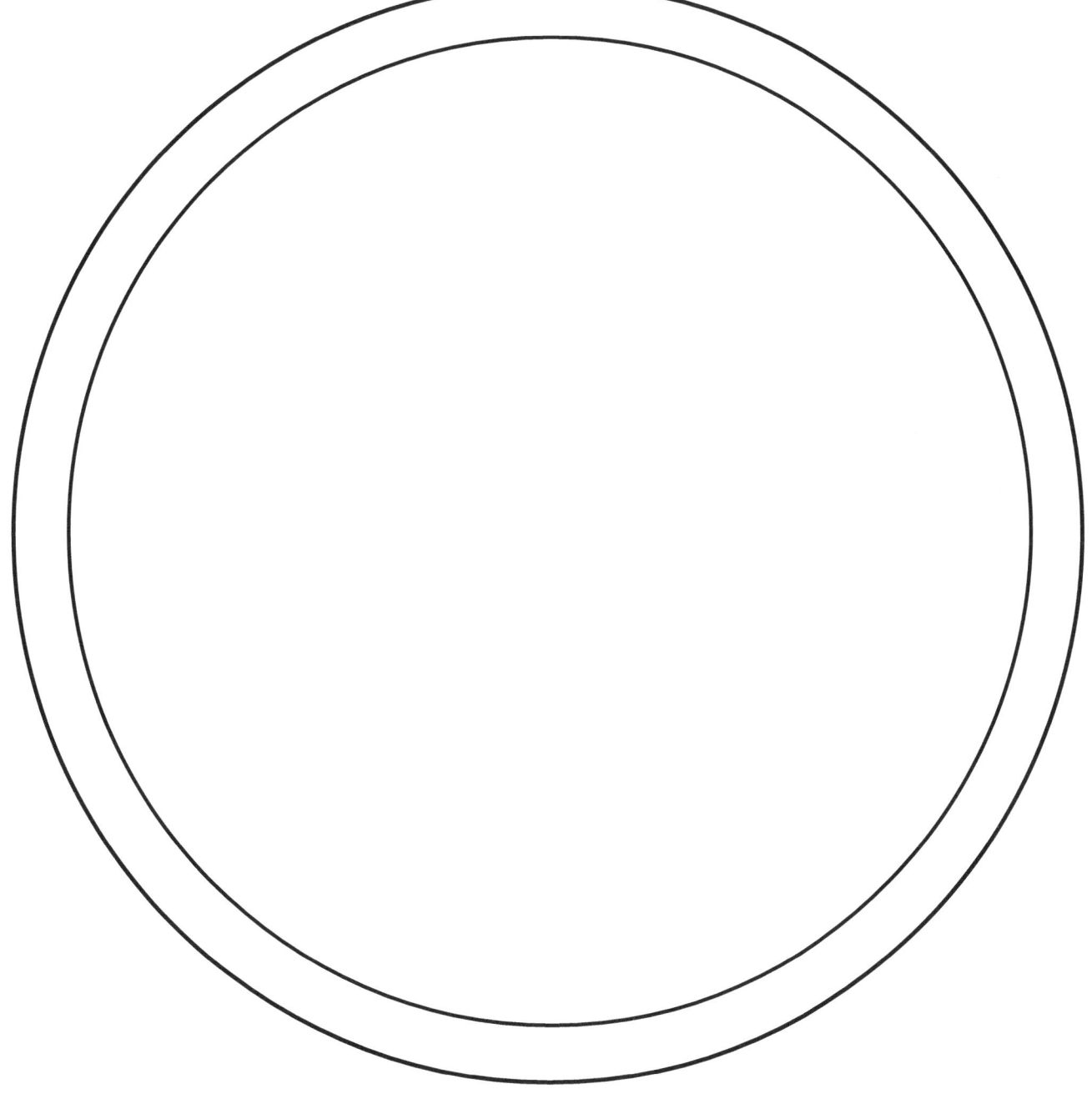

TEENS – DISCOVERING IDENTITY AND MOVING TOWARD INDEPENDENCE

My Storm
FOR THE FACILITATOR

I. Purpose
To adopt a calm mindset amidst a chaotic situation.

II. Skills
Describe a difficult or stormy personal situation and the related thoughts, feelings and actions
Document one or more positive thoughts, feelings and actions related to the same situation.
Re-create a calm eye of the storm using imagery and words.
Identify four or more different types of emotional storms and one or more ways to cope with each.
Compose one or more sentences that a personified *calm in the center of the storm* would say.

III. Possible Activities
  a. Plan to use the three *My Storm* handouts during the same or consecutive sessions.
  b. Ask teens to share ideas about experiences with bad weather and storms.
  c. Plan to distribute the handouts one at a time. Complete each handout before the next is presented.
   - *My Situation Part I*, page 81.
     A volunteer reads the FACT aloud and encourages reactions.
     Another volunteer reads the directions aloud.
     Allow time for completion.
   - *My Situation Part II*, page 82.
     A volunteer reads the directions aloud.
     Allow time for completion.
     Encourage teens to share responses to *My Situation*, *Parts I and II*, and receive peer feedback.
     Elicit that some situations may not change, but outlook, emotions and behavior, can be productive.
   - *My Calm Place*, page 83.
     Volunteers read the information and directions aloud.
     Allow time for completion.
     Encourage teens to share their responses and receive peer feedback.

IV. Enrichment Activities
  a. Encourage teens to brainstorm types of storms not already addressed, and ways to cope.
     Possibilities
       - A distressing diagnosis – seek a second opinion, research reliable resources, find support.
       - A failing grade – ask for tutoring, stick to a homework schedule, find online study resources.
       - A break up – recognize you will love again, believe the next relationship may be better.
       - Gossip about you – Know that people who really care about you will not believe lies.
  b. Encourage teens to imagine what the *calming words in the center of the storm* might say to them.
     Possibilities
       - I'm always here for you.
       - Your peace comes from within.
       - Replace panic with possibilities.
       - Remember past obstacles you overcame.
       - The universe speaks to you.

IDENTITY AND INDEPENDENCE 7

In the progress of personality, first comes a declaration of independence, then a recognition of interdependence.
~ Henry Van Dyke

Codependent? .... page **87** ▶
Teens identify signs of healthy and/or unhealthy levels of dependence in personal relationships. Teens discuss ways to break the cycle of codependency.

Altruism .... page **89** ▶
Teens are encouraged to develop altruistic passions and develop action plans. Teens state ways to overcome possible obstacles, and learn about advocacy and altruism opportunities by playing "Connectedness Clue."

WHAT INFLUENCES TEENS? .... page **93** ▶
Teens make decisions about role models and behaviors to emulate. Teens play "What If" and share what they would do in situations similar to news stories about famous people's actions.

"OH, THE PLACES YOU'LL GO!" .... page **97** ▶
Teens are motivated and empowered toward positive self-direction as they analyze and personalize a Dr. Seuss quotation. Teens compose silly stories about motivation, goals, and challenges.

AUTONOMY .... page **99** ▶
Teens recognize that peer influences usually decrease as teens advance toward adulthood. Teens play "Advice Anonymous" and ask for, listen to, and evaluate advice, and then make their decisions.

The Art of Negotiation .... page **103** ▶
Teens demonstrate negotiation skills in parent/caregiver situations involving independence-related privileges. Teens brainstorm safety rules that are non-negotiable.

TEENS – DISCOVERING IDENTITY AND MOVING TOWARD INDEPENDENCE

Chapter 7 – Identity and Independence Skills

Throughout the chapter, teens will communicate through oral, written, and graphic expression, and give and receive feedback.

Teens: Skills in each activity.
Facilitators: Competencies to evaluate.

Codependent?
- Compare a relationship to an addiction cycle in descriptions of the following: Discomfort when not in contact. No natural "high" without the person. Putting the person above self. Feeling desperate without the person. Needing the person, solely to be without pain. Withdrawal (depression, anxiety), and craving a fix (to be with the person).
- Document whether the relationship shows signs of healthy dependence or unhealthy codependence.
- Identify ten or more signs of codependency.

Altruism
- Offer an opinion about a journal entry writer's altruistic passion after reading two entries.
- Identify a current experience that could become an altruistic pursuit.
- Identify one way to carry out twenty-eight or more pursuits.
- Guess twenty-eight or more altruistic categories from peers' descriptions of related activities.
- Identify two preferred ways to advocate from among four options.
- Develop an action plan to pursue a personal passion.
- Identify two or more personal benefits of altruism.
- Research and report on organization(s) that encourage and aid teens in community service.

What Influences Teens?
- List five or more positive and negative behaviors of people in the public eye.
- Describe three or more behaviors to emulate.
- Share personal decisions to eight hypothetical situations similar to recent news stories.
- Create two scenarios for peers to state what they would do to respond to peer scenarios.
- Describe a personal role model's qualities.
- Describe three personal actions that would positively influence others.
- Brainstorm ten or more positive ways to make life more exciting, versus focusing on others' lives.

"Oh, the Places You'll Go!"
- Analyze an excerpt and apply six concepts that promote personal choice.
- Compose a message about motivation, goals, challenges, etc., while having fun with words.

Autonomy
- Give two or more personal examples of increased peer influence in early teens compared to earlier childhood, and increased self-influence as teens move toward adulthood.
- State one or more pieces of evidence of increased self-reliance regarding emotions, values, and actions.
- Ask for and receive advice. Hear and evaluate opinions. State an independent decision.
- Stand up and express personal beliefs in response to one or more questions.

The Art of Negotiation
- Practice negotiation skills: ask for a privilege, anticipate adult reactions, state one or more ways responsibility has been indicated, suggest two or more compromises.
- Identify trusted adults who may mediate in teen-parent/caregiver disagreements.
- Give four or more examples of non-negotiable issues.
- Verbalize concepts about win-win, mediation, respect, and never acting out or covertly defying a ruling.
- Brainstorm compromises for self and peers to present to parents/caregivers about current conflicts.
- Identify two or more circumstances in which negotiation and mediation are used outside the family.

Identity and Independence

Codependent?

> **FACT**
> Healthy dependence promotes mutual trust, safety, emotional closeness, and growth.
> Energy and effort are two-sided.
> Both people in a relationship give and take somewhat equally.
> They respect each other's beliefs and values.

Codependence is excessive dependence in a relationship with a partner, best friend, relative, or others.

You give too much power to the other person and diminish yourself.
A person becomes your drug of choice, similar to addiction.
You need frequent fixes (contact, affirmation, etc.).

See if this cycle applies to a current relationship.

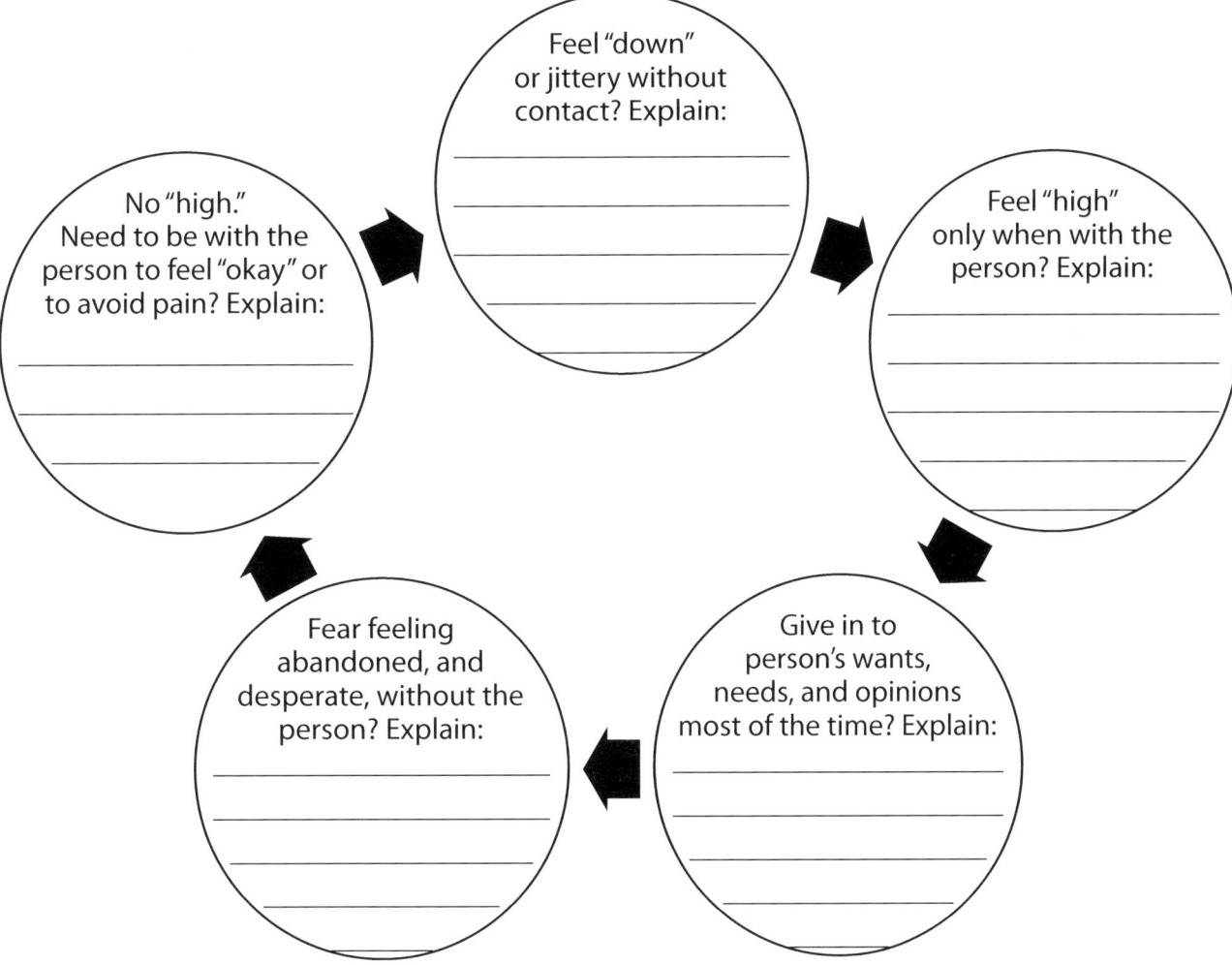

- Feel "down" or jittery without contact? Explain:
- Feel "high" only when with the person? Explain:
- Give in to person's wants, needs, and opinions most of the time? Explain:
- Fear feeling abandoned, and desperate, without the person? Explain:
- No "high." Need to be with the person to feel "okay" or to avoid pain? Explain:

Did you discover healthy dependence or codependence? _____

TEENS – DISCOVERING IDENTITY AND MOVING TOWARD INDEPENDENCE

Codependent?
FOR THE FACILITATOR

I. Purpose
To identify signs of healthy and/or unhealthy levels of dependence in a personal relationship.

II. Skills
Compare a relationship to an addiction cycle by describing the following:
- Extent of discomfort when not in constant contact.
- Level of exhilaration felt only with the person. No natural "high" without the person.
- Frequency of putting the person above self.
- Anticipated intensity of abandonment and desperation to be felt without the person.
- Loss of intense "high." The level of need to be with the person, solely to be without pain.
- The emergence of *withdrawal* (depression, anxiety), and cravings for a *fix* (to be with person).

Document whether the relationship shows signs of healthy dependence or unhealthy codependence. Identify ten or more signs of codependency. Identify ten or more ways to break the cycle.

III. Possible Activities
a. Ask "How do you try to gain independence from your parents/caregivers?" (Individual responses).
b. Ask "How much independence do you want in a close relationship?" (Individual responses).
c. Distribute the *Codependent?* handout. A volunteer reads the FACT aloud and encourages responses.
d. Other volunteers read the information and directions aloud. Allow time for completion.
e. Encourage teens to share responses and receive peer feedback. Expect a variety of individual responses.
f. Encourage teens to brainstorm signs of a codependent relationship. A volunteer lists their ideas.

Possibilities
- You care much more about the relationship than the other person does.
- Your identity is tied into being part of a relationship.
- An unreturned text or call ruins your hour or day.
- You mentally build this person up and put yourself down.
- You're jealous when this person spends time with friends.
- You suffer in advance with intrusive thoughts of this person with another person.
- You're obsessed with this person's every want and move.
- You've lost touch with who you are and want to be, where you are going, and how you feel.
- You compromise your values, and keep opinions quiet, just to keep this person happy.
- You hold onto the relationship at all costs.
- You tolerate abuse (physical, emotional, sexual, and/or verbal.)

IV. Enrichment Activities
Encourage a discussion about the following ways to break the cycle of codependency:
- Recognize and admit that signs are present.
- Know that you will find a mutually satisfying, equally invested relationship, in the future.
- Discuss with a trusted adult.
- Talk with this person about the behaviors you will stop, and ways you want to be treated.
- The person may understand and comply with your wishes, or the relationship may end.
- Realize you are human. Do not beat yourself up mentally for codependent behavior.
- Realize you may feel a sense of loss from the separation. Know you will move forward.
- View the situation as an opportunity to re-connect with yourself.
- Beware, in the future, if you start to give too much time, effort, and affection, and the other person gives too little.

Identity and Independence

Altruism: What's Right In Front of Me?

> **FACT**
> An estimated 55% of youth, ages 12-18, participate in volunteer activities.
> Typically each spends 29 hours a year in volunteer activities.

Altruism is concern and motivation to help others without reward or recognition.
Your passion, what really matters to you, is a big part of your identity.
It may lead to a career, or hours of free-time enjoyment.
Sometimes you don't realize that it's right in front of your nose!

Read the following 16-year-old's journal entry.

Last week, I got in trouble. I was walking with Pat between classes.

As Pat entered the restroom we said our goodbyes.

As the restroom door closed, a teacher who does not know me, accused me of looking into the restroom.

As I tried to explain, my English teacher came up to us and stuck up for me, saying "I know this student would never do such a thing."

Afterward, my English teacher asked if I wanted to be a peer helper for a student with a disability.

I felt honored and said "Yes."

Now everyday instead of study hall, I work with this new friend.

Ten years later…

I continued my relationship with Pat for a few years.

The bigger picture? I am now a Vocational Rehabilitation counselor, helping people overcome challenges.

What sparked the journal entry writer's passion?

_____

_____

_____

What is right in front of you that might spark your passion?

_____

_____

_____

_____

TEENS – DISCOVERING IDENTITY AND MOVING TOWARD INDEPENDENCE

Altruism: Connectedness

> **FACT**
> Feeling connected to others, even by just reading words like "community" and "relationship" makes us more altruistic. In one study, when toddlers simply saw two dolls facing each other in the background of a photo, they were three times more likely to be helpful than when they saw the dolls in other poses.

Your passion helps you connect with people and/or causes.

Connectedness Clue Game Instructions

- Cut out each box below.
- For each category, write a clue about how to connect with the people, animals or cause.
- Do not use the actual word. *Example: Literacy – Do not say "teach at the library." You might say "help kids learn to read."*
- People will guess the category from your literacy clue.
- You may cross out categories you are not using and write in your own.
- When it is your turn, you will read your clue aloud.
- You may need to give additional clues until someone guesses the category.

Animal welfare	Bullying prevention	Education	Literacy	Environment
Physical health	Mental health	Addiction recovery	Homelessness	Hunger
Military/ veterans	Poverty	Peace	Family	Blended families
Foster families	Group homes	Gang violence prevention	Dating violence prevention	Child abuse prevention
Sexual orientation issues	Cultural diversity	Suicide or harm prevention	Sports	Art
Music	Theater	Writing	Place of worship	Incarcerated person's family

Identity and Independence

Altruism: My Action Plan

> **FACT**
> Budget cuts threatened an elementary school's music program. Middle and high school students formed a volunteer organization to provide weekly music lessons for the kids.

You can foster your independence by exercising free choice about what to do and how.

Think about your altruistic options.

What's My Passion?

What lifts my mood? _____

What energizes me? _____

What makes my time fly? _____

What tugs at my heart? _____

What do I prefer?
Circle the words in each pair that best describes you.

I prefer to work …

In A Team   or   Alone
Up Front   or   Behind the Scenes

My Action Plan

I've decided to pursue this passion _____

_____

I will find more facts about this by _____

_____

I will overcome my time issues by _____

_____

I will overcome financial issues by_____

_____

If I seem to lack some needed skills, I will_____

_____

If people say "It can't be done" I will _____

_____

I can get help to carry out this plan from _____

_____

My mindset for this plan needs to be _____

_____

TEENS – DISCOVERING IDENTITY AND MOVING TOWARD INDEPENDENCE

Altruism
FOR THE FACILITATOR

I. Purpose
To develop altruistic passion, an expression of identity.
To exercise independence by formulating an action plan.

II. Skills
Give an opinion about a journal entry writer's altruistic passion after reading two entries.
Identify a current experience that could become an altruistic pursuit.
Identify one way to carry out twenty eight or more pursuits.
Guess twenty eight or more altruistic categories from peers' descriptions of related activities.
Describe a personal passion by responding to four questions.
Identify two preferred ways to advocate from among four options.
State a personal altruistic passion.
Document an action plan by completing eight sentence-starters.
Identify two or more personal benefits of altruism.
Research and report on one or more organizations that encourage and aid teens
    in community service.

III. Possible Activities
a. Plan to present the three *Altruism* handouts during the same or consecutive sessions. Have scissors available.
b. Write "Altruism" on the board. Ask teens the definition (to help others without expecting any reward).
c. Distribute each handout separately, completing one before providing the next.
   What's Right In Front of Me?
   - A volunteer reads the FACT aloud and encourages reactions.
   - Another volunteer reads information and game instructions aloud.
   - Allow time for completion.
   - Encourage teens to share their individual responses and to receive peer feedback.
   Connectedness
   - A volunteer reads the FACT aloud and encourages reactions.
   - Another volunteer reads information and game instructions aloud.
   - Allow time for teens to cut out the boxes and write their responses.
   - Remind teens that their clues cannot contain the category's title word(s).
   - Prompt teens to play the game.
   My Action Plan
   - A volunteer reads the FACT aloud and encourages reactions.
   - Another volunteer reads information and game instructions aloud.
   - Allow time for completion.
   - Expect a variety of individual responses.
   - Encourage teens to share their responses and to receive peer feedback.

IV. Enrichment Activities
a. Ask "In what ways do people benefit from volunteering?"
   Possibilities
   - Learn how organizations work, meet people, overcome shyness or self-centeredness.
   - Acquire experience to help gain college admission and/or employment.
b. Motivate teens to research and report on organizations that promote altruism and advocacy.

Identity and Independence

WHAT INFLUENCES TEENS? FAMOUS PEOPLE

> **FACT**
> Celebrity-ism is a multi-million dollar pastime. Every time you turn on the TV, listen to music, surf the Internet or read the news, you see superstars. Media often treats them like royalty, and they are often imitated.

Consider well known people in entertainment, politics, sports, etc.
List as many behaviors and actions as possible that you have heard about some famous people.

Harmful Famous people's behaviors and actions that can influence others in a harmful way.	Helpful Famous people's behaviors and actions that can influence others in a positive way.

Which list was easier to create? _____

Which list is longer? _____

If a famous person does something, does that make it okay? _____

Why does it matter to us what famous people do? _____

_____

_____

List three famous people and one of their behaviors you may want to imitate.

1. _____
2. _____
3. _____

WHAT INFLUENCES TEENS? WHAT IF?

> **FACT**
> After infancy, the brain's most dramatic growth spurt occurs in teen age years. They are developing advanced reasoning – a logical thought process that can now handle hypothetical situations and answer the question "What if …?"

What would you do if …?

After a game, the opposing team's players start fighting with your friends.
This thought enters your mind: *"That popular athlete fights."* What would you do?
_____

You drank at a party and need to drive home.
This thought enters your mind: *"That certain celebrity drives under the influence."*
What would you do?
_____

You want to cheat on your partner.
This thought enters your mind: *"Famous people cheat on their partners."* What would you do?
_____

You are offered illegal drugs to change your body image.
This thought enters your mind: *"I could have that superstar's body."* What would you do?
_____

You're in an argument with your partner and feel like lashing out.
This thought enters your mind: *"A certain icon was accused of domestic violence."*
What would you do?
_____

You are asked to help end poverty. Some celebrities do it.
This thought enters your mind: *"They have the money to help. I don't."* What could you do?
_____

You've been sober six months. You're asked to share your recovery. Some stars reveal addiction.
This thought enters your mind: *"I'm not famous. No one wants to hear my story."*
What could you do?
_____

You're asked to help teach a skill at a children's day camp. Some talented people teach others.
This thought enters your mind: *"I'm not good enough to teach kids."* What could you do?
_____

On the *back* of this page, create two situations for others to answer:
"What would you do if …?"
_____

Identity and Independence

WHAT INFLUENCES TEENS? POSITIVE ROLE MODELS

> **FACT**
> Studies show that teens usually select sports and pop stars, parents or caregivers, teachers or others in the community as positive role-models.

My positive role model is …

_____

_____

because …

_____

_____

_____

_____

I hope to be a positive role model for …

_____

_____

_____

_____

by these actions …

_____

_____

_____

_____

TEENS – DISCOVERING IDENTITY AND MOVING TOWARD INDEPENDENCE

WHAT INFLUENCES TEENS?
FOR THE FACILITATOR

I. **Purpose**
   To decide independently about role models and behaviors to emulate.
   To be aware of how famous people influence teens.
   To make independent decisions in situations that resemble celebrity news stories.

II. **Skills**
   List five or more positive and negative behaviors of people in the public eye.
   Describe three or more behaviors to emulate.
   Share personal decisions to eight hypothetical situations similar to recent news stories.
   Create two scenarios for peers to state what they would do.
   Respond to two or more peer-created scenarios that require independent thinking.
   Describe a personal role model's qualities.
   Describe three personal actions that would positively influence others.
   Brainstorm ten or more positive ways to make own life more exciting, versus focusing on the lives of others.

III. **Possible Activities**
   a. Plan to present the three *What Influences Teens?* handouts during the same or consecutive sessions.
   b. Before the session, select preferred formats below.
   c. At the start of the session, ask teens to share thoughts of celebrities in entertainment, sports, politics, etc.

   ***Famous People*, page 93. Team Format – Recommended**
   - Distribute the handout to all teens. A volunteer reads the FACT aloud and encourages reactions.
   - Another volunteer reads the information and directions aloud.
   - Divide the group into two teams – the Harmfuls and the Helpfuls.
   - Secretaries for each team record their teams' lists and responses to the questions.
   - The group re-convenes. Secretaries read their teams' responses aloud.

   ***What If*, page 94. Game Show Format – Recommended**
   - A volunteer reads the FACT aloud and encourages reactions.
   - Give one copy of the handout to the host at this time.
   - The host will read the scenarios one at a time and call on volunteers to share what they would do.
   - Tell teens to provide solution-oriented responses – what they would do and how they would do it.
   - After the game, distribute the handout to all teens who will write their own scenarios on the back.
   - Teens read their scenarios aloud. Peers respond.

   ***Individual Format for both*: *Famous People*, Page 93 *and What If*, Page 94.**
   - Distribute the handout. Volunteers read the FACTs aloud and encourage reactions.
   - Another volunteer reads the information and directions aloud.
   - Allow time for completion.
   - Encourage teens to share their responses and receive peer feedback.

   ***Positive Role Models*, page 95.**
   - Distribute the handouts to all teens. A volunteer reads the FACT aloud and encourages reactions.
   - Allow time for individual completion.
   - Encourage teens to share responses and to receive peer feedback.

IV. **Enrichment Activities**
   Suggest that the next time teens are overly focused on a famous person, ask this question:
   "How could I add positive excitement to my life?"
   Possibilities
   Try a new hobby, class, club, exercise, sport, skill.
   Read a good book. Create a story, work of art, craft, blog, poem, etc.

"OH, THE PLACES YOU'LL GO!"

> **FACT**
> Dr. Seuss (Theodor Seuss Geisel – 1904-1991) wrote and illustrated forty-six children's books that have been translated into fifteen languages and sold more than two hundred million copies. "Oh, the Places You'll Go!" spikes in sales every spring because so many people give the book to high school and college grads.

You have brains in your head.
You have feet in your shoes.
You can steer yourself any direction you choose.
You're on your own.
And you know what you know.
And YOU are the one who'll decide where you'll go.

~ Dr. Seuss

What does this quotation by Dr. Seuss mean to you at this point in your life?

_____
_____
_____
_____
_____
_____
_____
_____
_____
_____
_____
_____
_____
_____
_____
_____
_____
_____

TEENS – DISCOVERING IDENTITY AND MOVING TOWARD INDEPENDENCE

"OH, THE PLACES YOU'LL GO!"
FOR THE FACILITATOR

I. Purpose
To motivate and empower positive self-direction.

II. Skills
Analyze an excerpt and apply six concepts that promote personal choice.
Compose a message about motivations, goals, challenges, etc. while having fun with words.

III. Possible Activities
a. Ask teens about the Dr. Seuss books they read when they were younger.
b. Explain that there is one book often given to high school and college graduates.
c. Distribute the **Oh, the Places You'll Go!** handout.
d. A volunteer reads the FACT aloud and encourage reactions.
e. Another volunteer reads the directions aloud.
f. Allow time for completion.
g. Encourage teens to share their responses and receive peer feedback.
h. Expect a variety of individual responses.
i. Suggest that the group put a personal spin on each line.
   Possibilities
   You have brains in your head. Use them! Think about possibilities. Consider consequences.
   You have feet in your shoes. You have the power to walk toward or away from people, places and things.
   You can steer yourself… With visualization and inspiration. By evaluating advice and options.
   You're on your own. Your decisions are increasingly independent as parents/caregivers relinquish control.
   And you know… Where you've been, where you go and don't want to go, who/what can help or hurt you.
   You are the one who'll decide… To overcome obstacles, to seize opportunities, work toward a goal.

IV. Enrichment Activities
a. Explain that Dr. Seuss wrote **Green Eggs and Ham** on a dare. His publisher bet he couldn't write a book using only fifty different words. To make learning to read fun for the kids, he wrote a silly story about a picky eater and a person who wouldn't take "No" for an answer.
b. Suggest that individuals or teams compose silly stories using no more than fifty different words.
   Possible Topics
   • Challenges
   • Decisions
   • Directions
   • Goals
   • Heads
   • Hands
   • Hearts
   • Independence
   • What people know (the past and present)
   • What people do not know yet (the future)

Identity and Independence

AUTONOMY – DIAGRAM

> **FACT**
> "Autonomy" comes from Greek roots.
> "Auto" means "self". "Nomos" means "law" or "custom."
> The person who seeks autonomy wants to make decisions independently.

Young to Middle Teen Years
Peer influence (dependence on peers) usually increases compared to childhood.

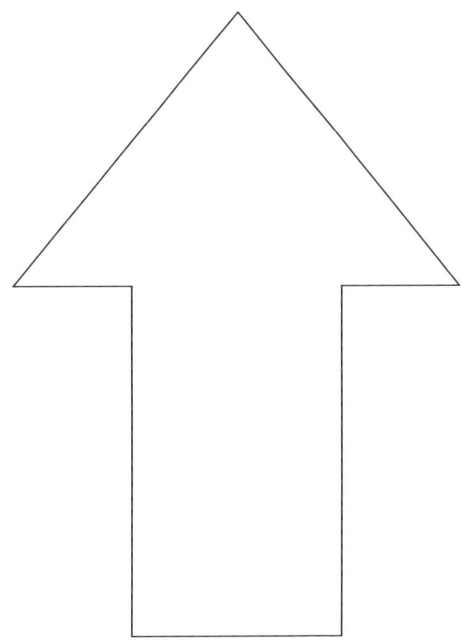

Late to Post-Teen Years
Self-influence (autonomy) usually increases as teens move toward adulthood.

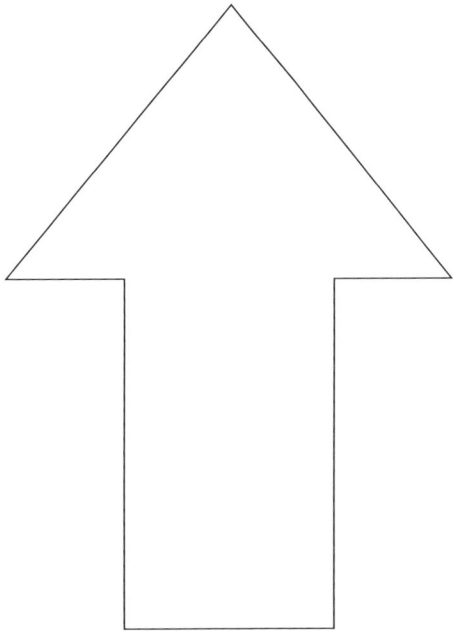

TEENS – DISCOVERING IDENTITY AND MOVING TOWARD INDEPENDENCE

AUTONOMY – DIAGRAM DIRECTIONS

Write in each arrow on the *Diagram* page.

1st Arrow Pointing Up
Share two or more ways your peers influence you more than when you were younger.

2nd Arrow Pointing Up
Share two or more ways you influence **yourself** more now than when you were younger.

Autonomy grows throughout adulthood whenever you need a new level of self-reliance.

Three types of autonomy affect emotions, values and actions.

I'm beginning to rely more on myself and less on my peers when it comes to:

These emotions …

_____

_____

_____

_____

These values (ethics, politics, spirituality, and other beliefs) …

_____

_____

_____

_____

These actions …

_____

_____

_____

_____

Identity and Independence

AUTONOMY – ADVICE

> **FACT**
> Everyone seeks advice at one time or another. Identical sisters, Esther and Pauline Friedman became two of the most famous syndicated newspaper advice columnists – Ann Landers and Dear Abby. People ask advice and remain anonymous using a name that represents them. (for instance - Signed, Confused)

An autonomous person …
Asks trusted people for advice.
Does not blindly follow advice.
Weighs the pros and cons and makes a well thought-out decision.

Advice Anonymous Game
In the box below, write about a real or imaginary situation in which a teen might ask advice.
  Sign with an anonymous name that describes the situation.
  Tear or cut out the letter.
  Fold the letter and place it in the container that will be passed around.
  Players will take turns pretending to be the letter-writer and the advisor.
When you play the person who is asking for advice …
  Select a folded letter.
  Open and read the letter aloud, pretending you have that situation.
  Call on two or more volunteer advisors.
  Hear their advice.
  Weigh the pros and cons.
  Make your decision and share it.
When you are the advisor …
  Listen to the letter.
  Do NOT ask any questions of the letter-reader.
  Give your advice solely on the information provided in the letter.
  The person reading the letter may or may not take your advice. It is that person's choice.

Dear Advisor,
I need advice about …

Yours truly, _____

TEENS – DISCOVERING IDENTITY AND MOVING TOWARD INDEPENDENCE

AUTONOMY
FOR THE FACILITATOR

I. **Purpose**
   To recognize that peer influence usually decreases as teens advance in age.
   To practice autonomy.

II. **Skills**
   Give two or more personal examples of the following:
      Increased peer influence in early teens compared to earlier childhood
      Increased self-influence as teens move toward adulthood
   State one or more evidences of increased self-reliance in each of these categories:
      Emotions, Values, and Actions
   Ask for and receive advice. Hear opinions and weigh the pros and cons.
   State an independent decision.
   Stand up for personal beliefs physically, and respond verbally to one or more questions.

III. **Possible Activities**
   a. Plan to present the three *Autonomy* handouts during the same or consecutive sessions.
   b. Ask teens "What's the favorite word of toddlers going through the *Terrible Twos?* (No).
   c. Explain that teens go through a similar stage in which they often say No to adults.
   d. Ask "What are the No's all about?" (Exerting independence and autonomy).
   e. Distribute the first two *Autonomy* handouts:
      Autonomy Diagram, page 99, and *Autonomy Diagram Directions*, 100.
      - *Autonomy Diagram*
         A Volunteer reads the FACT aloud and encourages reactions.
         Another volunteer reads the arrow information aloud.
      - *Autonomy Diagram Directions*
         Review the directions with teens. Allow time for completion of the diagram page and journaling.
         Encourage teens to share their responses and to receive peer feedback.
         Expect a variety of individual responses.
      - *Autonomy Advice*
         Distribute the handout. A volunteer reads the FACT aloud and encourages reactions.
         Another volunteer reads the information and game instructions aloud.
         Allow time for teens to complete brief letters. Teens tear or cut and fold their letters.
         Provide a container. A volunteer collects the letters.
         Quickly scan the letters for appropriate content. Remove letters as needed.
         Invite teens whose letters are not read to meet with you afterwards.
         Teens play the game. Remind advisors to ask no questions of the teens who read the letters.
         Advisors may ask peers for help, depending on the issues and time.

IV. **Enrichment Activities**
Play Ask the Audience
   - Cut out the list of questions below. Provide the list to teens as they take turns playing talk show host.
   - The host reads a question aloud. Volunteers raise hands to respond.
   - The host walks up to the seats of volunteers. Volunteers stand up and respond to the questions.

Questions for *Ask the Audience*

What do you stand for?
Who do you stand with?
Where do you stand on a controversial issue?
Who decides who you are?

What do you value?
What action would you like to take, on a controversial issue?
What do you believe?

Identity and Independence

The Art of Negotiation

> **FACT**
> Science confirms a neurochemical is released in the brain when wants or needs are threatened, and that makes people want to either fight or avoid the situation. But, there is no neurochemical for negotiation. Negotiation requires effort and the decision to deal with the situation and to consider compromise.

Practice the art of negotiation
Respond to the steps. Anticipate what your parent/caregiver might say.

You: A privilege I'd like is …

___

___

Adult might say:

___

___

You: I believe I have shown responsibility to handle the privilege by …

___

___

Adult might say:

___

___

You: Would you consider a compromise? (Suggest one or more possible compromises).

___

___

___

TEENS – DISCOVERING IDENTITY AND MOVING TOWARD INDEPENDENCE

The Art of Negotiation
FOR THE FACILITATOR

I. **Purpose**
   To demonstrate negotiation skills in parent/caregiver situations involving independence-related privileges.

II. **Skills**
   Practice negotiation skills:
   Ask for a privilege.
   Anticipate adult reactions.
   State one or more ways responsibility has been displayed.
   Suggest two or more compromises.
   Identify trusted adults who may mediate in teen-parent/caregiver disagreements.
   Give four or more examples of non-negotiable issues.
   Verbalize concepts about win-win, mediation, respect, and never acting out or covertly defying a ruling.
   Brainstorm compromises for self and peers to present to parents/caregivers about current conflicts.
   Identify two or more circumstances in which negotiation and mediation are used outside the family.

III. **Possible Activities**
   a. Write "Negotiate" on the board. Ask its meaning. (Reach an agreement or compromise through talk).
   b. Encourage teens to share experiences with both negotiation and compromise.
   c. Explain that negotiation skills may help teens resolve independence issues with parents/caregivers.
   d. Distribute *The Art of Negotiation* handout.
   e. A volunteer reads the FACT and encourages reactions. Another volunteer reads the directions aloud.
   f. Allow time for completion.
   g. Encourage teens to share their responses and receive peer feedback.
   h. Expect a variety of individualized responses in the dialogue section.
   i. Ask teens in what situations they may need a mediator (if parents refuse to negotiate).
   j. Encourage teens to identify people who may mediate (adult relatives, counselors, social workers).
   k. Ask how teens would respond to persons who say compromise is "giving in" or "selling out" (it's a way for both parties to get a portion of their desired outcomes).
   l. Encourage teens to brainstorm rules that are non-negotiable.
   Possibilities
   - No use of mind-altering substances
   - No unsafe driving
   - No illegal activities
   - No dishonesty or other unethical behaviors

IV. **Enrichment Activities**
   a. Write these riddles on the board. Ask teens to guess the missing words.
      - What two three-letter words say "There are no losers in compromises"?
        _____ - _____ (win-win).
      - What technique can be used when negotiation has been unsuccessful?
        ____ ____ ____ ____ ____ ____ ____ (mediate).
      - What "R" word describes what people should show each other during negotiations?
        ____ ____ ____ ____ ____ ____ ____ (respect).
      - What NOT to do if you're dissatisfied with the outcome? (Act out, sneak behind their backs).
   b. Suggest that teens role play situations in which they ask for privileges, and parents/caregivers resist.
   c. Ask teens to brainstorm compromises for teens to present to their parents/caregivers.
   d. Prompt teens to identify other situations in which negotiation and mediation are helpful (with friends, employers, etc. On a broader scale, between political parties, and among nations).

DAILY SKILLS MATTER 8

Every artist was first an amateur.
~ Ralph Waldo Emerson

Money Matters .... page 107 ▶
Teens develop a budget for spending, saving, and sharing, and learn about types of money accounts and credit issues. Teens discuss the emotional aspects of money.

Time Matters .... page 111 ▶
Teens implement time-management techniques, and estimate amounts of time spent working toward future goals. Teens identify emotions that reduce productivity.

Safety Matters .... page 115 ▶
Teens research and report ways to avoid being crime victims in public, at home, and online. Teens explore street smarts, wisdom on wheels, privacy, and other ways to remain safe.

Job Matters .... page 121 ▶
Teens acknowledge ways to obtain and retain employment. Teens note how entry level jobs help them prepare for careers, even in different lines of work.

Career Matters .... page 123 ▶
Teens identify personal factors and occupations to consider. Teens review types of work in professional, skilled, technical, military, and other service opportunities.

Food Matters .... page 127 ▶
Teens demonstrate knowledge about food safety through TV chef spoofs. Teens play "What Would You Do with This Food?" about dilemmas.

Safe Driving Matters .... page 129 ▶
Teens learn to refuse to ride with reckless drivers by writing potentially dangerous scenarios and responding to "What can I do?" Teens create safe driving bumper stickers.

Health Matters .... page 131 ▶
Teens are helped to develop healthy habits and awareness of health care needs. Teens prepare health-fair stations addressing nutrition, exercise, hygiene, and health check-ups.

LIFE MATTERS .... page 133 ▶
Teens learn to tell a trusted adult if anyone wants to harm self and/or others. Teens identify thoughts, feelings, or struggles that indicate the need for help.

Chapter 8 – Daily Skills Matter Skills

Throughout the chapter, teens will communicate through oral, written, and graphic expression, and give and receive feedback.

Teens: Skills in each activity.   **Facilitators:** Competencies to evaluate.

Money Matters
- Document three or more facts about each: spending, saving, sharing, accounts, budgets, credit.
- Develop a monthly budget. Identify three or more emotional aspects of money management.

Time Matters
- Identify what's most important, what stands in the way, and five emotions that undermine goals.
- Estimate the number of interruptions experienced per day and how they interfere with productivity.
- Develop an Uninterrupted Quiet Time Contract to present to friends.
- Document time-management techniques already implemented, and new ones that may help.
- Develop a Time Plan for the upcoming twenty four hours. Use six or more suggestions.
- Identify ways time has healed emotional wounds, and promoted four types of growth.

Safety Matters
- Present eight tips to prevent victimization in public, homes, vehicles, on media, and around weapons.

Job Matters
- Link fourteen descriptors with each of three categories while playing a scavenger hunt game.
- Give personal examples about getting, keeping and/or losing jobs.
- Describe five or more ways entry level jobs help people prepare for future careers.

Career Matters
- From thirty six statements, select those that apply to personal interests, abilities, and preferences.
- Rank order four preferences: to work with data, people, things and ideas. Give reasons for choices.
- Identify attributes of public service, and ways to serve in government, non-profit, and military jobs.
- Research one or more occupations of interest: labor market trends, wages, education and training, etc.

Food Matters
- Discuss eighteen food handling guidelines. Apply food safety principles in a mock TV chef spoof.
- Create and respond to one or more What Would You Do with This Food? dilemmas.

Safe Driving Matters
- Compose two situations in which a teen may be tempted to ride with someone who drives recklessly.
- Identify two or more ways to handle unsafe driver situations composed by peers.
- Create one or more safe driving slogans or bumper stickers, in six words or less.
- Identify and discuss fifteen or more safe driving concepts.

Health Matters
- Identify components of a healthy diet and estimate recommended amounts.
- List ten or more questions to ask a physician about diagnoses, tests, medications, and surgery.
- Describe enjoyable ways to incorporate one or more hours of physical activity into each day.
- State three or more ways to practice good grooming and hygiene, dental and medical maintenance.

Life Matters
- Acknowledge that people who talk about harming self and/or others may follow through.
- Discuss the importance of telling a trusted adult if self/others may be in danger.
- Name three or more trusted adults. Identify twenty-four signs that warrant adult intervention.
- Note which signs are present in self or are suspected in someone close.
- Learn two phone numbers to call and a place to receive emergency help.
- Differentiate myth from fact by responding to three or more questions about misconceptions.

Daily Skills Matter

Money Matters: Spend, Save, Share

> **FACT**
> Chrometophobia is an abnormal and persistent fear of money. Sufferers experience undue anxiety even though they realize their fear is irrational. They worry that they might mismanage money or that money might live up to its reputation as "the root of all evil!"

I spend money on …

_____

_____

_____

_____

_____

I save money for…

_____

_____

_____

_____

_____

I share money by …

_____

_____

_____

_____

_____

Money Matters: The ABC's

> **FACT**
> According to studies, spending money on experiences instead of possessions, and on others rather than yourself, yields more happiness.

A = Accounts
Below, write everything you know about money accounts.

B = Budget
Below, write everything you know about budgets.

C = Credit
Below, write everything you know about credit.

Daily Skills Matter ▶

Money Matters: My Budget

A budget helps you come out ahead,
to spend and share less than you earn so that you can save.

		MONTHLY AMOUNTS
Income Monthly earnings		
	Job $ _____	
	Allowance $ _____	
	Other (gifts, etc.) $ _____	
	$ _____	
	$ _____	
Total Income	$ _____	
Monthly Necessities		
	Bills $ _____	
	Transportation $ _____	
	School supplies $ _____	
	Clothing $ _____	
	List other necessities $ _____	
	$ _____	
	$ _____	
	Total Necessities	$ _____
Monthly Fun		
	Electronics $ _____	
	Entertainment $ _____	
	Restaurants $ _____	
	Other Fun $ _____	
	$ _____	
	$ _____	
	Total Fun	$ _____
Total Spending (Necessities + Fun)		$ _____
	Total Income	$ _____
	Subtract Total Spending	$ _____
Monthly Savings before Sharing Total income minus spending	Savings Balance	$ _____
Monthly Sharing Decide on an amount of money to share each month, (*charity, organization, food kitchen, domestic shelter, etc.*)		$ _____
Money Leftover to Save	Monthly savings before sharing	$ _____
	Minus monthly sharing	$ _____
	Savings after sharing	$ _____

TEENS – DISCOVERING IDENTITY AND MOVING TOWARD INDEPENDENCE

Money Matters
FOR THE FACILITATOR

I. Purpose
To develop a budget for spending, saving and sharing.
To identify facts about accounts, budgets and credit.

II. Skills
Document three or more facts about each: spending, saving and sharing,
Document three or more facts about each: accounts, budgets, credit.
Develop a monthly budget.
Identify three or more emotional aspects of money management.

III. Possible Activities
a. Plan to present the three *Money Matters* handouts during the same or consecutive sessions.
b. Before the session, tape a few dollar bills to the board.
c. At the start of session, ask teens what money means to them.
d. Expect a variety of individual responses.
e. Distribute the handouts one at a time. Complete one before presenting the next.
   - **Spend, Save, Share**, page 107.
     A volunteer reads the FACT aloud and encourages reactions.
     Allow time for completion. Encourage teens to share responses and receive peer feedback.
     Additional concepts to discuss:
     Spend – The newest electronics are most expensive and may have technological problems. Wait until the price drops and the wrinkles are ironed out. Comparison shop.
     Save – Have money from your paycheck diverted automatically into savings.
     Pay yourself first (save before you spend). Learn about interest rates and investment risks.
     Share – Give money to a reputable, researched, faith-based or charitable organization.
   - **The ABC's**, page 108.
     A volunteer reads the FACT aloud and encourages reactions.
     Another volunteer reads the directions aloud.
     Teens may work in teams (A, B, and C) or individually. Allow time for completion.
     Encourage teams or individuals to share their responses. A volunteer lists ideas on the board.
     Teens copy new ideas onto their handouts.
     Possibilities
     Accounts – Savings, checking, certificates of deposit, retirement and investment accounts.
     Budget – List income and output. Consider ways to increase income and decrease expenses.
       Credit – Credit cards, and car and student loans, add up and accrue interest.
       Be cautious! Buy only what you can afford to pay off soon. Use one credit card. Beware of introductory interest rates that rise in a few months. Credit history affects job eligibility, buying cars, homes, etc.
   - **My Budget**, page 109.
     Allow time for completion. Encourage teens to share responses and receive peer feedback.

IV. Enrichment Activities
Encourage a discussion about the emotional aspects of money.
Elicit
- Some people spend money on items they do not need due to boredom or depression.
- Some people try to buy friends by spending too much on gifts and entertainment.
- Alternatives to overspending are to deal with the boredom with productive diversions.
- Seek help for depression.
- Find friends who want friendship, not materialism.

Time Matters: Pirates

> **FACT**
> Daylight Savings Time began as a concept by Benjamin Franklin in 1784
> who proposed waking people earlier on bright summer mornings
> so they could work more during the day and thus save candles.

Name a goal that is important to you. *(accepted in college, find a job, sing a solo in choir, become the quarterback)*

_____

Approximately how many hours a week do you spend working toward this goal? _____

**Pirates rob ships' treasures.
Your time is your treasure.**

What and who are the Pirates that "rob" your time? _____

_____

_____

_____

_____

_____

Describe how each Pirate below can rob time from you to achieve your goal.

Fear _____

_____

Feeling Overwhelmed _____

_____

Perfectionism _____

_____

Procrastination _____

_____

People Pleasing _____

_____

Time Matters: Interruptions

> **FACT**
> Some business schools and successful companies promote Uninterrupted Quiet Time. During the specified hours, people avoid phone calls, texts, in-person contact, social media notifications, etc.
> Productivity has risen remarkably!

How do interruptions interfere with your homework, time to think, creative projects, etc.?

_____
_____

Individually, you can set aside specific times to neither accept phone calls nor check messages, emails, social media, etc. And, perhaps, you can start a trend among your friends.

People who interrupt you, interrupt themselves, and are interrupted by others. You might be interrupting other people's time too!

Create a contract to present to your friends. Then, collaborate and come up with a plan.

My *Uninterrupted Quiet Time* Contract

The benefits of uninterrupted quiet time for all of us are_____
_____

I suggest that we each specify some time each day when we each won't connect. Our time frames may be different based on our schedules. We will not expect immediate responses during each other's quiet times. After our quiet time we get to re-connect!

Sign if you're in, along with some possible quiet times that will work for you.

Signature	Possible quiet times
Signature	Possible quiet times
Signature	Possible quiet times
Signature	Possible quiet times
Signature	Possible quiet times
Signature	Possible quiet times
Signature	Possible quiet times

Daily Skills Matter ▶

Time Matters: Organization

> **FACT**
> Did you know that a "jiffy" is actually 1/100th of a second?
> When someone tells you, do it in a jiffy, they don't mean it literally.
> They mean quickly.

**Place a check mark in front of the techniques you already use.
Draw a star in front of new suggestions that may help you do one
thing at a time, and do it well.**

_____ Decide on priorities, then do first things first. First means most important, not the first thing that you want to do.

_____ Do the things you don't want to do first; get them out of the way.

_____ Know that when you focus on what's important, some small stuff may suffer.

_____ "No" is the best time-management technique. Say it to others. Say it to yourself.

_____ Organize – use a calendar, planner, or *Things to Do* list.

_____ Keep your homework with you to work on while waiting for rides, in lines, at appointments, etc.

_____ Set aside a private time and place to work on projects.

_____ Perfectionism and procrastination go hand in hand. People put off starting because they can't do it perfectly.

_____ Instead of wasting the time by making excuses, just do it!

_____ Once you start, motivation and creativity will kick in.

_____ Ask yourself often "What's most important to do right now?" Then do at least some of it.

Organize a Time Plan for the next twenty-four hours. Use the back of this page.

Add 25% to the amount of time you think activities will take.

Leave wiggle room in your schedule – time for unexpected set-backs and delays.

Build *down-time* into your schedule – time to connect with others, play, think, create, and recharge.

Plan your homework schedule around your unique best learning times.
    Ex: Maybe you're better at math in the morning and more creative later in the day.

Allow enough hours for sleep to help you work smarter and more energetically.

Make time for FUN!

TEENS – DISCOVERING IDENTITY AND MOVING TOWARD INDEPENDENCE

Time Matters
FOR THE FACILITATOR

I. Purpose
To implement time management techniques.

II. Skills
Identify what's most important to accomplish and what stands in the way.
Describe how five emotions can undermine accomplishments.
Estimate the number of interruptions experienced per day and how they interfere with productivity.
Develop an Uninterrupted Quiet Time Contract to present to friends.
Document the number of time-management techniques already implemented and add new ones that may help. Use the twelve suggestions.
Develop a Time Plan for the upcoming twenty-four hours. Use six or more suggestions.
Identify ways time has healed emotional wounds.
Give one or more personal examples of emotional, social, intellectual and spiritual growth over time.

III. Possible Activities
a. Plan to present the three *Time Matters* handouts during the same or consecutive sessions.
b. At the start of the session, ask "What does it mean to have the time of your life?" (An extremely enjoyable experience). Explain that teens will be thinking about the value of time.
c. Distribute the handouts one at a time. Complete each before the next is presented.
   Pirates, page 111.
   • A volunteer reads the FACT aloud and encourages reactions.
   • Allow time for completion.
   • Encourage teens to share their responses and to receive peer feedback.
   • Expect a variety of individual responses
     Possibilities
     Fear – can paralyze and prevent starting a task or working toward a goal.
     Feeling overwhelmed – can cause people to give up, to try to multi-task which worsens stress.
     Perfectionism – causes procrastination, wastes time on unimportant details or re-doing work.
     Procrastination – puts people farther behind. The later the start, the later the finish. Worsens dread.
     People Pleasing – inability to say no to low priorities deters the accomplishment of high priorities.
   Interruptions, page 112, and **Organization**, page 113.
   • Volunteers read the FACTs aloud and encourage reactions.
   • Other volunteers read the information or directions at the top of the pages aloud.
   • Allow time for completion.
   • Encourage teens to share their responses and to receive peer feedback.
   • Expect a variety of individual responses.

IV. Enrichment Activities
a. Copy this quotation onto the board:
   "Time is a very healing place, one in which you can grow." ~ Denise Tanner
b. Promote a discussion about ways time has healed teens' emotional wounds.
c. Encourage teens to give examples of how they have grown over time:
   • Emotionally
   • Socially
   • Intellectually
   • Spiritually

Safety Matters: Street Smarts

FACT
People think most robberies occur at banks and convenience stores.
The largest number are "strong arm" robberies, against one person.

Independence requires navigation in the community, country, and/or world.
Think about ways to save lives and property when walking along streets, on campus, or in public places.

Share findings by creating a poster.

Present your poster and consider ways to spread the message.

TEENS – DISCOVERING IDENTITY AND MOVING TOWARD INDEPENDENCE

Safety Matters: Home Security

FACT
In 2012 there were an estimated two million burglaries and 35,000 robberies in homes. According to the FBI, a burglary occurs somewhere in the U.S. every 15.4 seconds.

Perpetrators may come to your door and pretend to need help, say they are doing a survey, ask you to sign for a package, or say they ran into your car, or other excuses. You open the door and they barge in. Perpetrators also pose as prospective roommates or people who want to rent your apartment, or show you a place to live.

Independence often involves living away from parents/caregivers.
Think about ways to stay safe at home and/or when seeking a roommate or an apartment.

Share findings by planning a public service message.

Present this message to peers and brainstorm where to take it further.

Daily Skills Matter

Safety Matters: Wise on Wheels

> **FACT**
> Improved security devices make it harder to break into a parked car, so car-jacking is an easy alternative in order to use a vehicle for a quick escape after committing a crime, or to sell the car or its parts.
> The worst reasons? To kidnap, rob, rape, and/or murder the occupants.

Independence often requires your own transportation, rather than reliance on parent/caregiver drivers.
Think about ways to prevent vehicle-related crimes.

With a few other teens, write a skit about how to avoid being a victim of a crime when in any kind of a vehicle.

Perform the skit for peers.

Safety Matters: Privacy

> **FACT**
> Identity thieves may pretend to offer you a prize, loan, vacation, apartment, government grant, etc. Then they ask you for your personal information to "qualify." Some work for businesses and steal identity on-the-job.

Independence often requires financial transactions, technology, and safeguarding your privacy.

Think about ways to prevent identity theft or Internet crimes against teens.

Write lyrics about safeguarding your privacy.

Share your lyrics with peers.

Daily Skills Matter

Safety Matters: Weapons

FACT
The Brady Campaign to Prevent Gun Violence reports that an average of 268 people are shot every day in America. That's 97,820 per year.

Independence requires you to plan ahead for weapon emergencies.
Think about ways to stay safe when lethal weapons are present.

Pretend you are a law enforcement officer. Plan a presentation for young children about dangerous weapons.

Give this presentation to your peers and brainstorm how you can get the word out.

TEENS – DISCOVERING IDENTITY AND MOVING TOWARD INDEPENDENCE

Safety Matters
FOR THE FACILITATOR

I. Purpose
To research, report and maintain personal and property safety in public, at home, and online.

II. Skills
Identify and present eight or more tips to prevent being a victim of crime:
On the street, at home, in vehicles, when using media, and if weapons are encountered.

III. Possible Activities
a. Distribute the five *Safety Matters* handouts. Individuals and/or teams select one handout.
b. Teens research and prepare their findings. The group re-convenes.
c. Teens read their FACTS aloud and encourage reactions.
d. Teens present their work, and receive peer feedback.

Possibilities:

Street Smarts, page 115.
Sign up for safety notifications and alerts in your neighborhood. Keep a charged cell phone on you at all times. Have taxi and emergency numbers on speed dial. Avoid stationary cars with occupants. Have keys in hand as you approach your car. Lock doors when in or out of your vehicle. Park in well-lit, non-isolated areas. Beware of a stranger who offers to accompany you. Do not stop to help someone in an isolated area - call 911 or your local emergency services number. Carry a personal safety alarm. Wear shoes you can run in. If you are being followed, go into a business, or ask to walk with a group, and call police. Take high visibility and well-traveled routes when walking or biking. Trust your instincts if a person or situation seems unsafe and get away. Access cash machines in daylight and in populated areas. When on a date or at a gathering, do not leave food or drink unattended. Never accept a ride from a stranger, someone you hardly know, or someone on drugs, or drinking.

Home Security, page 116.
Know neighbors. Look out for each other. Do not hide keys outside. Give a spare key to a trusted friend or family member. Lock doors and windows. Do not invite someone you just met into your home. Block sliding doors with a pole in the track. Keep flashlight and phone nearby. Look out a window or peep hole before opening a door. Have someone with you when you meet a prospective roommate or visit a place to live.

Wise on Wheels, page 117.
Keep doors locked. Keep valuables in the trunk. Never let a stranger help you if your car breaks down - call for help. Do not stop to help someone in a secluded area - call for help. If you hit something in a secluded area, do not get out to investigate - view the area from inside your car - call for help. To minimize break downs: inspect tires, do preventive maintenance, and be sure to have enough gas. Lock your bike's rear wheel and frame to a bike rack, wear a helmet, obey traffic rules, watch for cars, especially in driveways and parking lots, travel well-lit, populated routes.

Possibilities:

Privacy, page 118.
Do not give out personal information. Take mail to a post office rather than leaving payments in your mailbox for pick-up. Pay online with a credit card rather than a debit card. Use anti-virus software and firewalls. Shred financial documents before discarding. Keep passwords secret. Do not open any messages that ask you to confirm your password to fix computer problems. Notify credit bureaus and close accounts that may have been compromised.

Weapons, page 119.
If you come across a gun, do not touch it. Leave the area and tell an adult. If a friend wants to show you a gun, say "No" and leave the area. If you overhear a person talking about using a weapon, or you see someone with a weapon, tell a trusted adult immediately – you do not need to be concerned about being a snitch – you may save lives. Ask in advance before visiting people if their families own weapons, if they are kept unloaded, locked, and if ammunition is stored separately and locked - BB guns, air rifles, and paint ball guns can cause serious injury. The noise from cap guns can damage hearing (wear ear protection). Do not keep caps in your pocket where they can ignite. Drop a toy gun immediately if approached by the police, who may mistake it for a real gun.

IV. Enrichment Activities – Encourage teens to recruit local police to speak at school assemblies.

Daily Skills Matter ▶

Job Matters

> **FACT**
> Wasting time at work can get people fired.
> The biggest time waster: Using the Internet. Next biggest time wasters are: socializing with co-workers, sending personal texts or making personal phone calls, and taking prolonged breaks.

Scavenger Hunt Cutouts

Your Positive Traits	Your Job Seeking Skills	You're Fired
Responsible	Accurate application	Bad-mouth boss or company on social media
Team player	Research the company	Gossip
Hard worker	Dressed appropriately for interview	Complain without suggesting solutions
Punctual	If asked, turn weaknesses into a strength	Sleep at work
Focus on quality and quantity	Eye contact with interviewer and firm hand shake	Under the influence of substances
Get along With co-workers	Cell phone off during interview	Disrespectful to the boss
Willing to learn	Honest answers during interview	Lie to or steal from employer, co-workers, customers
Accept constructive criticism	Ask about duties during interview	Not a team-player
Adapt To change	Do not ask about money and time off until offered the job	Poor quality and/or quantity of work
Positive outlook	Do not put down or insult prior employer	Unhelpful to others
Problem solver	Share strengths when asked at interview	Refuse to follow orders or procedures
Rule follower	Network with friends and family when looking for a job	Falsify records
Regular attendance	Have names and phone numbers of references, diplomas, certificates, and I.D. with you	Waste time
Self-starter	Be early for the interview	Argue with, or disrespect people

© 2015 WHOLE PERSON ASSOCIATES, 101 W. 2ND ST., SUITE 203, DULUTH MN 55802 • 800-247-6789

TEENS – DISCOVERING IDENTITY AND MOVING TOWARD INDEPENDENCE

FOR THE FACILITATOR

I. Purpose
To acknowledge ways to obtain and retain employment.
To prevent being fired.

II. Skills
Link fourteen descriptors with each of three categories *(Your Positive Traits, Your Job Seeking Skills, You're Fired)* while playing a scavenger hunt game.
Give personal examples about getting, keeping and/or losing jobs.
Describe five or more ways entry level jobs help people prepare for future careers.

III. Possible Activities
a. Before the session decide on the Team Game or Individual Puzzle Format. See "d" below.
b. For either format ask a volunteer to read the FACT and encourage reactions.
c. At the start of the session, ask teens about their experiences with scavenger hunts.
d. Explain that teens will play a game about an aspect of independence: getting and keeping a job.

Team Game Format - Recommended
- Prior to the session, photocopy one of the *Job Matters* handouts.
- Cut out all boxes. Set aside category headings (column titles):
  Your Positive Traits, Your Job Seeking Skills and *You're Fired*
- Scramble the other cutouts and hide them around the room.
- Divide the group into three teams. Give each team a category cutout.
- Elicit examples for each category.
  Your Positive Traits: hard worker
  Your Job Seeking Skills: neat application
  You're Fired: yelled at the boss.
- Tell team members to hunt for fourteen cutouts that describe their category.
- Allow a specified number of minutes for the hunt.
- The group re-convenes and reads their cutouts aloud.

Individual Puzzle Format
- Distribute the *Job Matters* handout to all teens.
- Instruct teens to do the following:
  Cut out all boxes.
  Place the three category headings in a horizontal row toward the top of their work space.
  Place the other cutouts face down and scramble them.
  When the facilitator says "Go," teens turn over the cutouts and place them under the correct headings.
- Allow a specified number of minutes to complete their puzzles.
- Encourage teens to share their responses.

e. (The descriptors are in the correct columns on the handout. Their order does not matter.)

IV. Enrichment Activities
a. Ask volunteers to share ways they obtained, retained, and/or lost jobs.
b. Ask "How do entry level jobs help you prepare for a career, even in a different line of work?"

Possibilities
- Many skills are transferrable to different situations – speed, accuracy, time management.
- People skills are developed, and are essential everywhere.
- Co-workers may help with networking later, if you keep in touch.
- Supervisors can give you excellent references.
- Your bosses may become positive or negative role models for you when you become a boss.

Daily Skills Matter

Career Matters: Choices

> **FACT**
> You will spend more than 80,000 hours of your life working!
> Why not spend it doing something you enjoy?

Check the boxes in front of all of the statements that apply to you.

- ☐ 8 AM to 5 PM, Monday through Friday work schedule, is for me.
- ☐ A training program might be good for me.
- ☐ An apprenticeship program would be great.
- ☐ Any entry level job(s) for a while after graduation would be good.
- ☐ As a people person, I want to work with a lot of people.
- ☐ Being outdoors is most important.
- ☐ Brainstorming ideas is what I love to do.
- ☐ Community college looks appealing to me.
- ☐ Competition motivates me.
- ☐ Computers are my thing!
- ☐ Deadlines are essential for me
- ☐ Enjoyable to me is working with data
- ☐ Eventually, I want to be in a management position.
- ☐ Flexible hours and days of work will be best for me.
- ☐ Following in the footsteps of a family member is my dream.
- ☐ Good health benefits are a must.
- ☐ Helping people is vital to me.
- ☐ High earnings are the top priority to me.
- ☐ I work best independently.
- ☐ In a job situation, I need structure and good supervision.
- ☐ Job security is very important to me.
- ☐ Light lifting or sedentary work is a must.
- ☐ Moderate or heavy lifting is okay.
- ☐ Most imperative to me is a steady income.
- ☐ My immediate future holds a college degree and beyond if necessary,
- ☐ On-the-job training would be perfect for me.
- ☐ Our family business seems like the right choice for me.
- ☐ Owning my own business is in my future.
- ☐ Part of my job description must be travel.
- ☐ Re-locating to another geographic area is okay with me.
- ☐ Research is a huge interest to me.
- ☐ Self-motivation needs to be of use in my career.
- ☐ Some type of armed forces work or participation feels right to me.
- ☐ Team work is appealing to me.
- ☐ The work place close to where I will be living is my goal.
- ☐ Traveling for a year before making a career decision sounds perfect for me.
- ☐ Using my second language is a must.
- ☐ Working with things rather than people would be my choice.

**On the back of this paper, elaborate about the most
interesting insights you learned about YOU!**

TEENS – DISCOVERING IDENTITY AND MOVING TOWARD INDEPENDENCE

Career Matters: Categories

Rank order your choices. #1 = most liked. # 4 = least liked. Explain.

#ifndef _____ **Work with Data (Information)**

Because …

#_____ **Work with Things (Hands-On)**

Because …

#_____ **Work with People**

Because …

#_____ **Work with Ideas**

Because …

#_____ **Work with _____**
OTHER
Because …

#_____ **Work with _____**
OTHER
Because …

#_____ **Work with _____**
OTHER
Because …

#_____ **Work with _____**
OTHER
Because …

Daily Skills Matter

Career Matters: Service

Public service can be in government, civil service, non-profit, military, and many other occupations.

> I can assure you, public service is a stimulating, proud, and lively enterprise.
> It is not just a way of life, it is a way to live fully.
> Its greatest attraction is the sheer challenge of it —
> struggling to find solutions to the great issues of the day.
> It can fulfill your highest aspirations.
> The call to service is one of the highest callings you will hear and your country can make.
>
> ~ Lee H. Hamilton

Circle the word(s) above, by Hamilton, that you find most appealing about public service. Explain

___

In the future, if you feel you are called, how do you imagine yourself serving?

___

What does "to live fully" mean to you?

___

Career Matters

FOR THE FACILITATOR

I. Purpose

To identify personal factors and types of occupations to consider.

II. Skills

Select applicable statements about personal interests, abilities, preferences, etc. from among thirty six.

Rank order four preferences: to work with data, people, things and ideas. Give reasons for the choices.

Identify one or more attributes of public service described in a quotation.

Imagine and describe personal ways to serve in government, civil service, non- profit, the military, etc.

Describe the personal meaning of the phrase in the quotation, "to live fully."

Research one or more occupations of interest: labor market trends, wages, education and training, etc.

III. Possible Activities

a. Plan to present the three *Career Matters* handouts during the same or consecutive sessions.

b. Distribute the handouts one at a time. Complete one before the next is presented.
- *Career Matters:* Choices, page 123.
  A volunteer reads the FACT aloud and encourages reactions.
  Allow time for completion. Encourage teens to share their insights and to receive peer feedback.
- *Career Matters:* Categories, page 124.
  Allow time for completion. Encourage teens to share their responses and to receive peer feedback.
- *Career Matters:* Service, page 125.
  A volunteer reads the information and quotation aloud.
  Allow time for completion. Encourage teens to share their responses and to receive peer feedback.

IV. Enrichment Activity

a. Make one copy of this facilitator page. Cut on the broken line. Photocopy for all participants.

b. Allow time for completion. Encourage teens with similar choices to collaborate as they research.

c. Suggest that individuals and/or panels share their information with the group.

Circle any of the careers/jobs that you wish to learn more about and/or add your own.

Architecture and/or Engineering	Management
Arts and/or Design	Math
Building and/or Grounds Cleaning	Media and/or Communication
Business and/or Financial	Military
Community and/or Social Service	Office and/or Administrative Support
Computer and/or Information Technology	Personal Care and Service
Construction and/or Extraction	Physical and/or Mental Healthcare
Education, Training, and/or Library	Production
Entertainment and/or Sports	Protective Service
Farming, Fishing, and/or Forestry	Sales
Food Preparation and/or Serving	Teacher, Professor, and/or Researcher
Installation, Maintenance, and/or Repair	Transportation and Material Moving
Language	Other _____
Law	
Legal	Other _____
Life, Physical, and/or Social Science	Other _____

Choose one occupational group or specific trade/technical occupation to explore further. Use the United States Department of Labor's *Occupational Outlook Handbook* online and /or other resources. Document prospects for future employment, wages, education, training, and other info.

Daily Skills Matter

Food Matters

> **FACT**
> "Spoilage bacteria" (mold) can be seen smelled and tasted,
> but may not make you sick. "Pathogenic bacteria" cannot be seen, smelled or tasted.
> Yet, it makes you very sick.

**Preparing your own meals is a healthy, and thrifty, indication of independence. Right?
What could be wrong with protein from lean meat, poultry, fish and eggs?
Aren't fresh veggies loaded with vitamins?
Isn't reduced price food a great value?**

**Imagine you are TV Chef Sensation, however, you are ignorant of food SAFETY facts.
Create a cooking show spoof, in which you unknowingly do all of the WRONG things.
If you don't have props, either draw them or pantomime them, pretending
they are in front of you.**

Some helpful tips about the safe ways to handle food:

- Wash hands before and after touching food.
- Wash fresh fruits and vegetables in plain water.
- Cook meat, poultry, fish, and eggs thoroughly. Use a meat thermometer.
- Do not let raw beef, chicken, fish or pork come into contact with other foods.
- Don't use the same utensils or plate that was used for raw meat, for cooked meat, until all are washed.
- Wash cutting boards, knives and counter tops with soap or disinfectant.
- Check labels to see how soon to use or freeze fresh food.
- Thaw food in the refrigerator or microwave, not at room temperature.
- Keep cold foods cold and hot foods hot.
- Put leftovers away within two hours. Eat in three to four days or freeze.
- Never wipe your hands on a dish towel.
- Do not heat food in plastic margarine or cottage cheese containers. Melting releases toxic chemicals.
- Don't freeze foods containing mayonnaise or hard cooked eggs.
- If you wonder if a food is too old, remember the rule: "When in doubt, throw it out!"

When shopping:

- Put frozen and refrigerated foods in your cart last.
- Put plastic bags on meats, poultry and fish.
- Check expiration dates before buying food, especially if labeled "Reduced."
- Put refrigerated foods away first when you get home.

**When you're finished creating your Cooking Show spoof,
volunteer to present your program, alone or with your co-stars.**

TEENS – DISCOVERING IDENTITY AND MOVING TOWARD INDEPENDENCE

Food Matters
FOR THE FACILITATOR

I. **Purpose**
   To demonstrate knowledge about food safety.

II. **Skills**
   Acknowledge the difference between two types of bacteria: spoilage and pathogenic.
   Apply eight or more food safety principles through a simulated television show or video.
   Discuss fourteen food handling guidelines and four safe grocery shopping suggestions.
   Create and respond to one or more *What Would You Do with This Food?* stories.

III. **Possible Activities**
   a. Before session, gather some kitchen props, if available.
   b. Ask teens what they plan to eat when they move away from home
      (fast, frozen, home cooked food).
   c. Encourage a brief discussion about TV cooking shows and reality show chef competitions.
   d. Distribute the *Food Matters* handout.
   e. A volunteer reads the FACT aloud and encourages reactions.
   f. Other volunteers read the rhetorical questions, the *Imagine you are TV Chef Sensation*
      directions, and the helpful tips about correct food handling aloud.
   g. Suggest that some teens may choose to work alone.
      Others may choose to work or with partners or teams.
   h. Provide space for teens who are working together to confer and rehearse in corners of the
      room or hallway.
   i. Allow time for preparation.
   j. The group re-convenes.
   k. Individuals, partners and teams present their spoofs.
   l. When teens portray a spoof, ask the audience to make a list of all the wrong actions.
   m. Audience members identify the incorrect food handling procedures seen in spoofs.
   n. Audience members give feedback after the spoofs.
   o. Encourage a discussion about any helpful tips not addressed in the presentations.

IV. **Enrichment Activities**
   a. Encourage teens to make-up "What Would You Do with This Food?" stories.
   b. Teens take turns telling their brief stories.
   c. Peers respond.
      Possibilities
      • You are at a picnic. The potato salad looks delicious. It has been out of the cooler and on
        the table in the sun for two hours. What would you do with this food?
      • It's your first dinner party in your new apartment. You drain spaghetti. If accidentally goes
        down the disposal. You can retrieve it with your tongs. What would you do with this food?
      • You're barbequing for friends at your graduation party. Several cooked steaks fall to the
        ground. No one saw. What would you do with this food?

Daily Skills Matter ▶

Safe Driving Matters

FACT
The risk of motor vehicle crashes is higher among sixteen-to nineteen-year-olds than any other age group. In fact, per mile driving, sixteen-to nineteen-year-olds are nearly three times more likely than drivers twenty or older, to be in a FATAL crash.

What can you do if you are about to get in a car, or are riding with someone who is driving unsafely?

Example:
I get into the car with my uncle who is dropping me off at the movies. I can see that he is drunk. My friend is waiting for me in front of the movie theater. What can I do?

_____
_____

In each box, write a situation you have been in, or that a teen could encounter, regarding …
Riding (or not) with someone who is driving unsafely.
Cut or tear your paper on the broken lines.
Fold your slips of paper and put them into a container that will be passed around.
People will take turns reading the situations aloud and responding.

✂

Situation: _____
_____
_____
_____
_____

What can I do? _____
_____
_____
_____

✂

Situation: _____
_____
_____
_____
_____

What can I do? _____
_____
_____
_____

TEENS – DISCOVERING IDENTITY AND MOVING TOWARD INDEPENDENCE

Safe Driving Matters
FOR THE FACILITATOR

I. Purpose
To refuse to ride with people who drive unsafely.
To identify safe driving concepts.

II. Skills
Compose two situations in which a teen may be tempted to ride with someone who is driving unsafely.
Identify two or more ways to handle unsafe driver situations composed by peers.
Create one or more safe driving messages or slogans, in six words or less, that could be bumper stickers.
Identify and discuss fifteen or more safe driving concepts.

III. Possible Activities
a. Ask for a show of hands for the number of teens who have driver's licenses.
b. Ask for a show of hands for the number of teens who plan to get driver's licenses.
c. Distribute the *Safe Driving Matters* handout.
d. A volunteer reads the FACT aloud and encourages reactions.
e. Encourage teens to silently read, and respond in writing and/or orally, to the example situation at the top of the page. (Call someone else for a ride. Call the friend about the situation. Postpone the movie for a later time).
f. Allow time for completion of the situations. Collect slips of paper and place at the front of the room.
g. Teens take turns reading the situations aloud and responding to "What can I do?"

IV. Enrichment Activities
a. Tell teens to think about themselves as drivers.
b. Write "Say it in six words or less" on the board.
c. Prompt teens to create messages or slogans about safe driving that could become bumper stickers. *Example:* Adjust your speed to driving conditions.
d. Encourage teens to share their responses.
   Possibilities
   - Be especially careful at night.
   - Don't text and drive.
   - Have first aid kits in cars.
   - Never drink or drug and drive.
   - No racing.
   - Keep music low enough to hear sirens.
   - Never drive when drowsy.
   - Maintain adequate following distance.
e. Encourage teens to brainstorm other safe driving tips that may be longer than six words
   Possibilities
   - Be sure preventive maintenance is done (check oil, tires, brakes, fluids, windshield wipers, etc.).
   - Do not allow distractions (by passengers, pets, loud music, etc.)
   - Have supplies related to geography (drinking water when driving in the desert).
   - Have supplies related to the weather (blankets, rock salt, snow chains in winter).
   - Have emergency road service and auto insurance numbers accessible.
   - Look carefully in applicable directions, checking blind spots and mirrors before lane changes.
   - Prevent and/or know how to recover from skids and other emergencies.
   - Before starting the car, check mirrors and properly adjust them, if anyone else has driven the car.
f. Suggest a bulletin board display of their slogans and/or to make them into bumper stickers.

Daily Skills Matter

Health Matters

> **FACT**
> A health survey asked teens
> "Which best describes how you feel when you make healthy food choices?"
> The results:
> Good about myself and my choices – 43.6%
> Energetic and strong – 16.2%
> Satisfied and nourished – 16.2 %
> Deprived – 24%.

Volunteers will prepare a paper exhibit, and staff a station.
Your exhibit is the back of this page taped onto a wall.
Write your station's name at the top of your paper exhibit.
To "staff" your station, means to encourage visitors to add to your paper exhibit.

Dish Station
Draw a big circle (dish).
Divide it into four sections.
Draw a smaller circle where a glass would be.
Label the fourths: Fruit, Vegetables, Protein, and Whole Grains.
Label the smaller circle Dairy.
As people visit your station, ask them to write a food on a section.
After all your visitors leave, add some of your own suggestions.

Ask the Doctor Station
Divide your paper into three columns.
Label them Sick or Hurt, Test or Surgery, and New Medicine.
As people visit your station, ask them to write a question to ask a doctor in a column.
After all your visitors leave, add some of your own suggestions.

Exercise an Hour-a-Day Station
Divide your paper into three columns.
Label them: Team Sports, Individual Sports, and Daily Activities.
As people visit your station, ask them to write in one of the columns.
After your visitors leave, add some of your own suggestions.

Preventive Maintenance Station
Divide your paper into three columns.
Label them: Hygiene, Dental Care, and Physical and Mental Health Care.
As people visit your station, ask them to write in one of the columns.
After your visitors leave, add some of your own suggestions.

TEENS – DISCOVERING IDENTITY AND MOVING TOWARD INDEPENDENCE

Health Matters
FOR THE FACILITATOR

I. Purpose
To develop healthy habits.
To take responsibility for young adult health care needs.

II. Skills
Identify components of a healthy diet and estimate recommended amounts.
List ten or more questions to ask a physician about diagnoses, tests, medications, surgery.
Describe personal enjoyable ways to incorporate one or more hours of physical activity into each day.
State three or more ways to practice good grooming and hygiene, dental and
   physical health maintenance.
Define the intent of HIPAA legislation: to protect the privacy of health care information.

III. Possible Activities
   a. Before the session, have tape available or provide large sticky poster paper, and color markers.
   b. Ask teens to raise hands if they make their own doctor, dental, and/or hair cut appointments.
   c. Point out that to manage health care needs is important for independence.
   d. Distribute the *Health Matters* handout.
   e. A volunteer reads the FACT and encourages reactions.
   f. Other volunteers read the station descriptions aloud.
   g. Ideally, two or three teens will staff each station. One person may staff a station if necessary.
   h. Each station uses a wall or board space. Each posts one paper exhibit.
   i. The remaining teens will be visitors who rotate through the stations.
   j. Visitors make only one entry on each paper per rotation, but may go around as many times as possible until they have no new ideas to add.
   k. Teens who are staffing may rotate through other stations.
   l. After visitors are finished, staffers add their additional suggestions.
   m. The group re-convenes. Staffers read aloud and/or show their paper exhibits and receive peer feedback.
   Possibilities
   - **Dish Station** – expect a variety of healthy food choices.
   - **Ask the Doctor Station**
     Sick or Hurt: "The course of the condition?" "Diet or lifestyle changes?" "Contagious?" "Options?"
     Test or Surgery: "Preparation?" "Expected outcomes?" "Alternatives?" "Recuperation time?"
     New Medicine Station: "Generic?" "Interactions?" "Drowsiness?" "How long is it needed?"
   - **Exercise an Hour a Day Station** – expect a variety of sports and activities.
   - **Preventive Maintenance Station** – Hygiene and Dental Care – expect a variety of responses.
     Health Maintenance – concepts to elicit if not addressed by teens:
     Regular physical exams. If sexually active, medical visits regarding safe sex.
     Become established with a primary care MD before teens are no longer eligible for pediatrics.
     Explore health insurance before teens are no longer covered by their parents' plans.
     Check college, employer, private, and governmental affordable health care plans.
     A primary care MD can be an ally for physical, emotional, and/or substance related issues.
     A primary care MD will refer patients to specialists and/or programs.
     A primary care MD will address sports injury prevention, or refer to a sports medicine specialist.

IV. Enrichment Activities
Encourage teens to research HIPAA – Health Insurance Portability & Accountability Act.
Encourage a discussion about the intent and benefits of the Federal law that protects the privacy of health information: electronically, in writing, or in spoken form.

Daily Skills Matter

LIFE MATTERS

> **FACT**
> People who talk about harming others often harm others.
> People who talk about suicide often die by suicide.
> NEVER keep a secret if someone's life is in danger.

**At times, people experience unwanted thoughts, feelings, or struggles.
When the following feelings and behaviors disrupt one's life, or go on for too long,
there may be a bigger problem:**

- Afraid
- Angry
- Anxious
- Apathetic
- Burdensome
- Desperate
- Eating issues
- Grief

- Helpless
- Hopeless
- Hostile
- Inability to focus
- Lonely
- Manic
- Overly emotional
- Overwhelmed

- Paranoid
- Sad
- Sleepless
- Stressed
- Substance abuse
- Thoughts of death
- Trapped
- Urges to do harm

**If someone you know is having many of the feelings above
and/or is talking about harming him/herself or others:**

- Urge the person to tell a trusted adult immediately.
- If a person refuses to accept help, tell an adult immediately.

**If you are having many of the feelings above
and/or considering harm yourself or others:**

- **Tell a trusted adult.**
- **Call 911 or your local emergency services number.**
- **Go to the closest hospital Emergency Department, or call the National Suicide Prevention Lifeline: 1-800-273-8255 (TALK).**

NEVER KEEP A SECRET IF SOMEONE'S LIFE IS IN DANGER.

TEENS – DISCOVERING IDENTITY AND MOVING TOWARD INDEPENDENCE

LIFE MATTERS
FOR THE FACILITATOR

I. Purpose
To tell a trusted adult if anyone expresses the desire to harm self and/or others.
To identify thoughts, feelings, or struggles, that may indicate a bigger problem, and ways to seek help.

II. Skills
Acknowledge that people who talk about harming self and/or others may follow through.
Discuss the importance of telling a trusted adult if self/others may be in danger.
Identify twenty-four signs that warrant adult intervention.
Note which signs are present in self or are suspected in someone close to the teen.
Learn two phone numbers to call and a place to receive emergency help.
Name three or more trusted adults.
Differentiate myth from fact by responding to three or more questions about common misconceptions.

III. Possible Activities
   a. Distribute the *Life Matters* resource page.
   b. A volunteer reads the FACT aloud and encourages reactions.
   c. Other volunteers read different sections of the page.
   d. Ask teens to think about themselves or a person they think may have many of the unwanted thoughts, feelings, or struggles addressed on the page.
   e. Direct teens to write a code name for self or the person, then place a check mark on the applicable words.
   f. Encourage teens to share their concerns, without revealing the person's identity.
   g. Emphasize the importance of seeking help for self or the other person.
   h. Ask for examples of trusted adults (teachers, counselors, parents/caregivers, spiritual leaders, etc.).
   i. Advise teens to save the page for reference, phone numbers, etc.
   j. Explain that no person should try to assess or help a person on their own.
   Seek additional expertise.
   k. When the pages have been put away, reinforce comprehension by asking questions:
   Possibilities
   "What do we know about people who talk about harming themselves or others?"
       (They may do it).
    "What should you do if you or someone wants to hurt themselves or others?"
       (Tell a trusted adult).
   "Where can a person call or go for help?"
       (911, National Suicide Prevention Lifeline, emergency room of a hospital or urgent care.)
   "What are some thoughts, feelings, or struggles that suggest someone needs help?" (See list).
   l. Depending on the facilitator's familiarity with the subject, and the teens' needs, the thoughts, feelings, and struggles may be further explored.

IV. Enrichment Activities
Ask these questions to clarify often misunderstood concepts:
   • "Do you betray a friend if you tell an adult they may be in danger?" (No. You may save a life).
   • "Do people who threaten suicide or homicide just want attention?" (No. Take them seriously).
   • "If someone seems *down*, should you ask if they are thinking about self-harm?" (Yes.)
     Explain that some people do not ask because they fear putting ideas in the friend's head.
     A person who is suicidal already has the idea.
     A person who is not suicidal will not be influenced by the question.

Whole Person Associates is the leading publisher of training resources for professionals who empower people to create and maintain healthy lifestyles. Our creative resources will help you work effectively with your clients in the areas of stress management, wellness promotion, mental health and life skills.

Please visit us at our web site: **WholePerson.com**. You can check out our entire line of products, place an order, request our print catalog, and sign up for our monthly special notifications.

Whole Person Associates
800-247-6789